Contact:
Christian assemblies for primary schools

Redvers Brandling

Blackwell Education

Published by
Basil Blackwell Limited
108 Cowley Road
Oxford OX4 1JF
England

British Library Cataloguing in Publication Data

Brandling, Redvers
  Contact: Christian assemblies.
  1. Primary schools. Morning assembly
  I. Title
  377.14

ISBN 0-631-90481-6

Typeset in 10 on 12pt Times Roman
by Colset Private Ltd, Singapore
Printed in Great Britain
by TJ Press (Padstow) Ltd

Acknowledgements

I am, as always, grateful to the staff and children of Dewhurst St Mary School, Cheshunt. Not only have they been a receptive audience for all these stories, but they have been a source of both inspiration and information with their own presentations.

I am grateful to Mrs Irene Keen for the story entitled: 'The Disappearing Cake'; to Rev T Lewis-LLoyd for 'The House' and to Miss MT Vakatale of the Fiji High Commission for 'The Power of Prayer'.

The poem 'Maths gone wrong' by Geoffrey Simpson first appeared in *Assembly – Poems and Prose* by Redvers Brandling, Published by Macmillan, 1977.

It should also be mentioned that some of the stories and poems in this book have been used, heard and re-adapted several times in assemblies. In consequence their original sources are not remembered and if this has unwittingly caused the infringement of copyright, the author apologises and will correct this omission in future editions if notified.

Contents

Introduction

The Education Reform Act of 1988 requires all pupils in attendance at a maintained school to take part in a daily act of worship. This should be 'mainly of a broadly Christian character'.

This book is a flexible resource which will help schools meet this requirement. The following extract from an excellent pamphlet: *Collective Worship in Hertfordshire* seems particularly appropriate in any consideration of 'broadly Christian' assemblies:

> In achieving this meaningful act of worship it is important to distinguish between worship and ritual. Rituals such as prayer, hymns, readings from the Scriptures are means of worship not worship in themselves. Schools may feel that other means of worship are as valid. Such as: Stories and Readings; Dance and Drama; Prayer/Meditations; Creative silence; Songs/Hymns/Music; Sacred/Secular Readings; Artefacts and Natural materials; Children's contributions; Visual aids.[1]

The material in this book embraces most of these aspects. It is organised in three main sections:

Section A: Complete assemblies

This section is designed to be used as flexibly as possible. It provides assemblies which can be presented by one person; by a group or by a class. (Content, language level or local circumstances may determine which option you choose.)

Each assembly is set out as follows:

---

[1] *Collective Worship in Hertforshire*, Guidance for Schools, March, 1989. Ref: RE Adviser, County Hall, Hertford SG13 8DF.

1   A brief presenter's note, setting the context for what follows.
2   An introduction which leads naturally into
3   Core material – a story, poem or passage.
4   Supplements: a hymn suggestion, a prayer and 'The Bible says', which details appropriate Biblical material.
5   Class presentation ideas – this gives practical suggestions for varied approaches to the assembly material.

The assemblies are arranged in four groups:
● true stories
● poems and passages
● folk stories
● great Christians and Bible stories

This enables the presenter to use a series of related assemblies over a period of time.

The age range catered for is 7 to 12. Teachers will be able to adapt material where they feel this is necessary. This might include shortening or lengthening assemblies to suit specific needs. It may also be helpful at this point to refer to Section C (see below).

Section B: Plays for assemblies

This section contains five 'ready-made' assemblies for class presentation, which may be photocopied. They are arranged as follows:

1   **On an oil rig** (Autumn term)
2   **I was there** (Spring term)
3   **Should I?** (Summer term)
4   **Signposts**
5   **Labels**

The last two assemblies could be used equally well at any time of the year. Although all of these assemblies could be adapted to suit the whole junior school age range, it might be helpful to indicate age groups to which they are best suited for 'instant' presentations.

On an oil rig	Lower/Middle
I was there	Middle/Upper
Should I?	Upper
Signposts	Lower
Labels	Middle/Upper

Section C: Information for teachers
This section suggests some alternative ways of using the material in this book.

1 The School/Christian Year
This links the school year month-by-month with the main events in the Christian year. Included in each month's details are the numbers of class assemblies and assemblies which would be appropriate at this time. No assembly is used more than once in this section. *Notable dates* are listed for each month, with ideas for appropriate assembly themes.

2 Assembly groupings by theme
For teachers who may wish to pursue a theme in detail. The appropriate assemblies are grouped beside theme titles.

3 Assembly groupings by age
There is obviously a very big overlap, so any age indicators can only be general guidelines but this reference may be helpful for 'instant' use.

4 Sources
This section details organisations, and their addresses, which are helpful for assembly purposes.

Section A
Class assemblies

1 Footballer? Footballer!

Presenter's note
This is one of those inspiring stories where determination in the face of apparently insurmountable difficulties ultimately achieves success.

Introduction
When we are young, we all have dreams about what we want to be when we grow up. Seldom can anybody's dreams have seemed more remote than those of David Kelly. After all, if you can't walk you haven't got much chance of becoming a footballer . . . or have you?

Core material
The crowd packed into the stadium in Dublin was very pleased with the way the football international between the Republic of Ireland and Israel was progressing. The Irish team was winning comfortably; their centre-forward had already scored two goals.

Suddenly the ball landed in the Israeli penalty area once again. Then the crowd roared as it crashed into the back of the goal. David Kelly, the Republic's centre-forward, had scored his hat trick!

As he ran back to the centre circle, the speedy, sharp-shooting centre-forward might have thought back to . . .

'David, David! Stay where you are. Don't move an inch. We'll have you down in no time.'

His parents' cries came up to David from the ground. High above them, he reached for another branch of the tree. Then – crash! With a flurry of broken branches and swirling leaves, David fell to the ground. There was a dreadful crash as he hit the ground, then a scream of pain.

'He's broken his leg!'

David *had* broken his leg, but sadly that was only the beginning of his troubles. When his leg was being examined in the hospital, the doctors discovered that he was suffering from a rare disease.

'It's called Perthes' disease,' explained one of the doctors to David's anxious parents. 'It means that the bones of the leg don't grow properly.'

'But is there a cure?'

'The only cure is time, I'm afraid. It might be a very, very long time.'

That was the start of an ordeal that would have tested the courage of any adult – and this was a four-year-old child.

David's legs were put in a special cast which was joined by an iron bar to stop them moving. For a whole year he had to be carried everywhere by his parents. At school, he got round in a machine a bit like a mini go-kart.

After a year, the doctors said there was a slight improvement. David could now use crutches, but he had to wear special clothing with an iron chain joined to the back of his foot, holding his left leg.

By the time he was nine years old, David could walk again. But one leg was shorter, and he still needed regular hospital treatment. Despite all this pain, discomfort and inconvenience, David dreamed about what he wanted to be – a footballer.

At last David was finally rid of his crutches. He began to play football – and he was brilliant! He was spotted by a professional club and by the time he was 22 he was Walsall's leading goal-scorer. International caps soon followed, and then he transferred to First Division club West Ham United. Truly a case of 'Footballer? Footballer!'

Hymn
'He who would valiant be' (*Come and Praise* Vol 1, 44)

Prayer
Oh Lord, help us to learn from the courage, fortitude, patience and determination of people like David Kelly. Teach us to value our good fortune. Give us strength to bear times of disappointment, pain and misfortune.

Please God, help us. Amen

The Bible says
A man's spirit may sustain him in sickness, but if the spirit is wounded, who can mend it?

Proverbs 18:14

Class presentation ideas

Preparation
- Collect scarves, badges, pennants etc for local football club(s) and set up a display just before the assembly.
- Prepare two envelopes, clearly labelled as follows:
1 The story of a boy
2 The story of a young man
Inside each envelope should be the relevant part of the story.
- Audience and presenters (5–6) could enter to the accompaniment of some rousing music.

Development
When presenters and audience are in place, two children hold up the envelopes so that everyone can see them.

Presenter 1   My envelope says 'The story of a boy'
Presenter 2   My envelope says 'The story of a young man'
Each child then reads the contents of their envelope.

Presenter 1	What was the name of the boy?
The rest of the group answers:	David Kelly.
Presenter 2	What was the name of the man?
Answer	David Kelly.
Presenter 1	So it was the same person?
Answer	Yes.

All the presenters then turn towards the audience and ask:
What can we learn from this story?

2 Another child

Presenter's note
The files of organisations like *Save the Children* are full of thought-provoking stories. This is one of them.

Introduction
What did you have for breakfast? Do you know what's for lunch today? Have you ever felt *really* hungry? Have you ever gone for two whole days without anything to eat at all?

These questions make us think – and perhaps they make us realise how lucky we are. Not all children are so lucky, as the following story tells us.

Core material
Save the Children is a charity organisation which gives help to children in need.

In 1988 a lady called Dorothy was working as a volunteer helper in a refugee camp in Somalia. At this time hundreds of refugees had crossed the border of Ethiopia to try and escape a terrible drought and famine. Among them was a little boy called Daahir. Dorothy met him at the camp and spoke to him.

'Yes I am hungry,' he answered, 'but I did have something to eat two days ago.'

Daahir was desperately thin. His skin was dry and patchy. Gradually, Dorothy got the rest of his story.

He had been walking for a week, all by himself. His father was dead and his mother was back in Ethiopia with his younger brothers. He was looking for his uncles to tell them his mother needed help, but he couldn't find them. He was four feet seven inches tall but weighed only 82.6 kg (37.5 lbs). He was nine years old.

Dorothy and Daahir became friends, but she was very worried. Conditions were very bad in the camp and every night between ten and 20 people died.

'I must try and help this little boy and give him a better life,' thought Dorothy. Eventually, after a great deal of trying, she got Daahir into a government sponsored orphanage. Here things began to look better for him. He got regular meals and his weight reached 158 kg (72 lbs). He also began to read and write and he began to learn to do something he had rarely done before – laugh.

(Adapted from an article in *Linx*, the *Save the Children Fund* magazine)

Hymn
'Sad, puzzled eyes' (*Come and Praise* Vol 2, 74)

Prayer

Dear God, So often we say, 'not just now . . . in a minute . . . I'll do it later . . . when I have time . . .' Let us remember that for many children in need the time is NOW. Their neglected bodies can wait no longer. For them today is all-important, because for them there may not be a tomorrow. Let us pray for the work of Save the Children Fund. Please give their workers strength, skill and courage and inspire people to be generous.
Amen

The Bible says
Blessed are those who show mercy;
mercy shall be shown to them.
Matthew 5:7

Class presentation ideas
This assembly could focus on a 'Beginnings and Expectations' theme, with the story of Dorothy and Daahir introduced about two-thirds of the way through the presentation.

Divide presenters into two groups:

Group 1 shows the sort of start in life a child in the Western/Developed world might have. This could be done through drama, mime, pictures and artefacts . . .

Presenter Good food, cleanliness, a caring home, medical care, a safe environment and a good climate. All these give a child a good start in life. What sort of future might such a child expect?

Group 2 shows the sort of start a child in the Third or Developing World might have.

Presenter Famine, war, extreme heat or cold, no home, no running water or health care. What does the future hold for these children? Hunger, disease – even death.

Follow this with the story of Dorothy and Daahir, a story where all the 'beginnings' were wrong, but the expected sad ending did not come about because of caring people and charitable organisations. This encourages children to appreciate the importance of striving to give all children a good start in life.

Follow up
A useful follow up might be to read or take out a subscription to the children's magazine *Linx*. It comes from *Save the Children Fund*, Mary Datchelor House, 17 Grove Lane, Camberwell, London SE5 8RD. Apart from stories like the one told here this magazine also has a letters page, puzzles, news, fund raising ideas. Although aimed at children it is very useful for teachers too.

3 Special qualities

Presenter's note
This story is about conquering a handicap – in this case blindness.

Introduction
This morning's story is about making the most of whatever special qualities we have – no matter what the difficulties.

Core material
'Have you heard?'
'Isn't it dreadful?'
'Terrible, terrible – I can hardly believe it.'
The year was 843 and the people talking were Japanese.
They had just heard some terrible news. The governor of their province, a young man called Hitoyasu, who was admired by everybody, had suddenly gone blind.
'What will he do?'
'What *can* he do?'
Hitoyasu was still only 28 years old and he was certainly not a person who gave up easily.
'People seem to think I'm good at poetry and music,' he said to himself. 'Well, I may be blind but I can still spend my time doing these things . . . in fact I have a good idea . . .'
Hitoyasu's idea was a brilliant one. He realised that many blind people were very good musicians. He invited blind people from all over Japan to come and live and work in his palace in Kyoto. Soon the concerts of these blind people became famous all over the country.
Then Hitoyasu made another discovery. If blind people had such a skilful and delicate sense of touch, he thought, might they not also be good at massaging other people who suffered from aches and pains in their muscles and joints? Hitoyasu was right – they were very good at it indeed. So much so that the Emperor said only blind people would be allowed to do this job in future.
These events took place hundreds of years ago. But in Japan today blind people are still highly respected for their skills in music and massage.

Hymn
'The family of man' (*Come and Praise* Vol 1, 69)

Prayer
Dear God, Thank you for those people who see clearly the needs of others,

Thank you for the time, patience and kindness they show, Give us the strength never to feel sorry for ourselves.
Amen

The Bible says
Idle hands make a man poor;
busy hands grow rich . . .
Proverbs 10:4

One man wins success by his words;
another gets his due reward by the work of his hands . . .
Proverbs 12:14

A man's spirit may sustain him in sickness
Proverbs 18:4

Class presentation ideas
It might be appropriate to concentrate on the positive aspects of the story, to increase appreciation of the senses of sound and touch.

Begin with the introduction and ask two of the presenting children to read the story. As the theme develops, focus on our sense of hearing, and how much pleasure we get from listening to and making music.

Play some carefully-chosen excerpts of recorded and taped music. It would be ideal if some of the presenters could produce some recorder or percussion work of their own.

The sense of touch is more difficult to portray effectively in a large group. The presenters might enact some incidents of 'healing hands' related to the comments of the story.

Follow up
A useful address here might be: Royal National Institute for the Blind, 224 Great Portland Street, London W1N 6AA.

4 Youngest-ever hero

Presenter's note
This true story is about a very young hero – only two years old!

Introduction
Today's story is about a little boy and his mother, but in this case it is the child who looks after the adult.

Core material
The wheels of Paul's tricycle wobbled as he rode it over the uneven bumps on the garden lawn. It was a lovely warm August day and two year old Paul was thoroughly enjoying himself playing in the garden whilst his mother sunbathed in a deck chair.

'Mum,' he shouted, but Mrs Wilcox did not answer.

'Mum!'

There was still no reply so Paul went up to his mother and gave her a shake.

'She must be asleep,' he thought.

But no matter how much he shook her, Mrs Wilcox did not wake up. Paul realised that something must be wrong. His mother must be ill.

Jumping off his tricycle, Paul ran out of the garden as fast as he could. He opened the gate and raced to a neighbour's house where he knew his mother sometimes went.

Reaching up as high as he could he hammered on the front door. He shouted out at the same time too. It seemed as if the door was going to stay shut for ever. Then it opened and he recognised one of his mum's friends.

'Mummy's sick,' the little boy gasped anxiously. 'Very sick.'

The neighbour was as quick-thinking as Paul had been. Taking him inside with her, she called an ambulance.

When the ambulance arrived its crew found that Mrs Wilcox was unconscious. She suffered from a disease called diabetes and needed regular treatment. The ambulance crew raced her to hospital, where she received emergency treatment.

Within a very short time Mrs Wilcox had recovered completely. When she did so she heard how Paul had saved her life.

'I'm proud of him,' said Mrs Wilcox.

'You must be,' replied one of the ambulance crew, 'He must be the youngest hero ever!'

Hymn
'A still, small voice' (*Come and Praise* Vol 2, 96)

Prayer
Let us pray this morning for small children everywhere. Let their lives be free from sadness and fear. Let them enjoy good health, good homes, love and care.
Please God, hear our prayer.

The Bible says
I tell you this; unless you turn around and become like children you will never enter the Kingdom of Heaven. Let a man humble himself till he is like this child, and he will be the greatest in the Kingdom of Heaven.
Matthew 18: 1–4

Class presentation ideas
The core material of this assembly might be portrayed by the presenters in a series of FACT announcements, eg:

Fact 1   Diabetes is an illness where the sufferer has to have regular treatment. They can do this for themselves but if it is missed then they can become unconscious and die.

Fact 2   A lady called Mrs Wilcox suffered from diabetes. One day she was sitting in the garden while her two-year-old son played nearby.

Fact 3   . . .

Continue this until the story is completed. To conclude, the presenters could point out that in a caring society even the youngest has a part to play.

5 The disappearing cake

Presenter's note
This story is about the personal penalty we all pay for sly or wrong behaviour – a guilty conscience.

Introduction
Have you ever said to yourself – 'I would like more' for example, 'I would like more time to watch TV before I go to bed; I would like more pocket money; I would like more sweets.'
  This morning's story is about a boy who thought he would 'like more'.

Core material
Think about your absolute favourite food for a few seconds. What is it? Chips? Ice cream? Fried rice?
  This morning's story is about a boy whose favourite food was chocolate cake. Let's call him Wayne. Wayne's family was very poor and he had lots of brothers and sisters. Every few weeks his mother made a special chocolate cake for all the family. Wayne looked forward to this with mixed feelings – he loved chocolate cake but there was never enough.
  Wayne's mother would put the cake on the table and then carefully cut it into sections – all the same size so that each person could have the same amount. One day Wayne's mother made one of her lovely cakes and left it on the pantry shelf.
  Wayne was putting the bread away after supper when he saw the cake there. He knew it would be cut up for tea tomorrow . . . but what if he could sneak a bit tonight? It looked so delicious.
  When everyone had gone to bed Wayne crept downstairs. He had a brilliant idea! He knew how he could get a really big piece of cake without anybody noticing any was missing. He was a genius!
  Ten minutes later Wayne was back in bed, feeling very pleased with himself.
  At teatime next day there stood the cake in the middle of the table, sliced into exactly the same number of pieces as usual. Wayne's brothers and sisters all sat around and took a piece and so did he.
  'Great, mum.'
  'Lovely cake.'
  'But there doesn't seem as much as usual.'
  'Funny that, because there are the same number of pieces as always.'
  'Well,' said Mrs Parkins, the children's mother, 'it's strange you should say that, because when I came down this morning I found the bread knife in the pantry with bits of chocolate cake sticking to it . . . but there were no pieces missing from the cake.'

Wayne felt his face getting redder and redder. He had forgotten about the knife! How could he have been so stupid?

'What's the matter, Wayne?' asked his mother. 'You're looking very hot and bothered.'

'Well . . . you see . . . I mean . . . *I* did it.'

'Did what?' asked mother relentlessly.

'I took some cake last night.'

'But how could you? There were no slices missing.'

'I . . . got the bread knife and I very carefully sliced the bottom off the cake so that nobody would notice.

'Well that was very clever of you Wayne, but it meant that everybody else got less than they should have done.'

Nobody else spoke, but Wayne suddenly felt that what he had done was not clever at all. Perhaps there were other words for it like 'selfish', or 'greedy'.

Hymn
'A still, small voice' (*Come and Praise* Vol 2, 96)

Prayer
Dear Lord, help us to realise that one person's gain is often another person's loss. To be greedy or selfish may mean that someone else does not get their fair share. Help us to see this and to act unselfishly at all times.

Amen

The Bible says
If you have a grievance against anyone, forgive him.
Mark 11: 25

Class presentation ideas
This assembly could be dramatised as follows. If there is a curtained area in the hall, position all the characters in the drama behind the curtains, with the household 'set' in place in front of them. The narrator sets the scene by commenting on how much the family enjoyed their chocolate cake. The characters portray this and then withdraw behind the curtain.

The narrator continues: 'Later that night . . .'

'Wayne' mimes slicing the bottom off the cake, adding some 'sotto voce' comments to clarify his actions. (If stage lighting and hall curtaining are available, this scene could be acted with appropriate lighting.)

Characters mime the final scene. The narrator finishes:

'I hope you will never be tempted to be greedy like Wayne'.

6 Colin to the rescue

Presenter's note
The courage of 'the man next door' is often inspiring because it calls for exceptional behaviour in a familiar, everyday environment.

Introduction
Look around you for a moment. What do you see? Well-known faces, well-known things, all just as you would expect it to be. But what if something very unexpected and very frightening suddenly happened? Today's story is about just such a situation. One minute everything was normal and routine, but the next . . .

Core material
'There's smoke coming out of that window!'
One of Colin Hunt's workmates pointed a stubby finger at a nearby house, as another wisp of smoke puffed out of an upstairs window. The two men were working on a building site in Cheshunt.
'You're right,' replied Colin, 'and . . .'
He didn't finish what he was going to say because another surge of smoke from the window was pierced by a glint of flame.
'Quick!' shouted Colin. 'It's a fire. We've got to get a move on!'
Seizing a ladder he rushed towards the high garden wall which separated him from the house. As he ran, he shouted over his shoulder,
'Somebody call the fire brigade – I'm going to get the folks out!'
One of Colin's workmates rushed to a telephone. Meanwhile, Colin was already climbing the garden wall. Once on the other side he could see more flames and hear the cries of children. Shouting for all he was worth, he burst into the house. He picked up tiny Stewart and Lisa Page and rushed them to safety. This disturbed the rest of the family, who had all been asleep, and they too dashed out of the house. Soon the fire brigade arrived. Although the house was badly damaged the Page family were safe and sound, thanks to Colin.
Months later, on Thursday 6 April, 1989, there was a special ceremony in Broxbourne Borough Council offices in Hertfordshire. Present were Colin, the Page family, a local councillor, two very senior police officeres and two senior fire brigade officers. Colin was awarded a special bravery certificate. One of the senior officers said:
'He acted instantly, and with great risk to himself. The children owe their lives to him.'

Hymn
'When I needed a neighbour' (*Come and Praise* Vol 1, 65)

Prayer
Oh Lord, so often we are slow and hesitant because we think too much about ourselves. Help us to awake to the needs of others. Give us the courage, speed and resourcefulness to take positive action.

Dear Lord, help us. Amen

The Bible says
Prepare yourself for testing.
Set a straight course, be resolute,
Do not lose your head in time of disaster.
Eccelesiasticus 2: 1–2

Class presentation ideas
This story could be adapted for a class or group presentation as follows:

Preparation
- Clear a small area, clearly visible to the audience – this is 'Broxbourne Council Offices'.
- Prepare a suitable 'bravery award' certificate.

Development
The 'action' takes place at the award ceremony. Children take the parts of the various people involved in the incident. One of the presenters takes the role of 'roving reporter' and interviews those concerned, eg

Reporter Tell me, Mrs Page, when did you realise that something was wrong?

Mrs Page Well, it was when Colin burst into the house shouting 'Fire!'

and so on. Finally, the reporter concludes the interview by saying:

Reporter We now know that the fire was accidentally started by young Stewart Page, who set fire to some bedding . . .

Follow up
The issue of fire precautions and safety in the home could be developed in a number of ways. It might be possible to invite a police or fire officer to come and talk to the children.

7 Saved

Presenter's note
This is really a story in three parts: the boys who were anxious to do the right thing; the girl whose life was filled with dread; the happy ending. It is another story where 'good' ultimately defeats 'evil'

Introduction
This morning's story is about a group of children who find a girl hiding in a ruined house. Why is she there? Listen to the story and you will find out.

Core material
'We've got to help her,' said Luigi.'There's no avoiding it.'

'She says she doesn't need help,' answered another boy.

'She's scared they'll send her back home,' said a third.

The group of boys were standing outside a derelict house near Venice in Italy. Behind the crumbling shutters and broken-down front door, a 15-year-old girl crouched on the floor of one of the rooms. Earlier they had talked to her.

'My name is Belinda,' she had said. 'I've run away from home.'

'Why?' Luigi had asked.

'Because my stepmother treats me like a slave. She beats me and keeps me locked in an airing cupboard. The only way I can stay alive is to steal food from the kitchen when she's not looking.'

'Are your family poor?'

'No, my father's rich and my stepmother drives a big American car. I only got away because my father gave me a little money for my fifteenth birthday present. When I escaped and got to this house it bought me some food. But there's none left now . . . and I can't . . . I can't . . .'

The girl hadn't been able to continue for crying, but when Luigi and his friends offered to help she begged them not to, fearing she would be returned to her slave's existence.

'Come on,' said Luigi finally, 'We'll take her to hospital. They'll know how to help there.'

So the boys persuaded Belinda to go with them. The doctors at the hospital were horrified at Belinda's condition, but with care and attention she soon made a complete recovery. Then her story became known. Soon newspaper readers all over Italy knew of what had happened to Belinda. Her cruel stepmother and father were put in prison for the way they had treated her. The story had a wonderful ending; Belinda's real mother was found in Australia. Far from having to return to her tortured existence in the airing cupboard, Belinda was soon flying to Australia to start a new life with her mother. All because a group of boys had insisted on doing what they felt was right.

Hymn
'Give us hope Lord' (*Come and Praise* Vol 2, 87)

Prayer

Father we thank you for the night
And for the pleasant morning light,
For rest and food and loving care,
And all that makes the world so fair.
Help us to do the things we should,
To be to others kind and good,
In all we do, in all we say,
To grow more loving every day.
Amen

The Bible says
How blest are those who hunger and thirst to see right prevail.
Matthew 5:6

Be humble always and gentle. Be forbearing with one another and charitable.
Ephesians 4:2

Class presentation ideas
This is a true story, but there are many folk tales where children suffer at the hands of selfish adults, eg 'Cinderella'.

The group could act out one or more of these familiar tales to remind everyone that stories so often reflect some aspect of real life.

This might then lead on to the point that Jesus told many stories for this very reason. This could be linked with examples of parables, or with assemblies using Biblical themes (see pages 119–141).

8 The Power of Prayer?

Presenter's note

This story of survival is inspiring from both a personal and a collective viewpoint.

Introduction

There are many things in life which we do not fully understand. The story which follows was told to the author of this book by Miss MT Vakatale, Deputy High Commissioner of the Fiji High Commission in London. The calm London office in which Miss Vakatale sat, seemed a very, very long way from the island on which the story took place, but the storyteller's thoughts were obviously far away 'at home' as she told this remarkable tale.

Core material

Taraivosa was a girl who lived in the village of Somo-Somo on the island of Gau in Fiji. There was great excitement in the village one day – a fishing trip was being organised.

'Can I go, please?' Taraivosa asked her father and mother.

'Well, I don't know.' replied her father. 'It's about 20 miles out to the reef. Who will look after you while you're out there?'

'No-one needs to look after me Father, after all I'm nearly 14. I'll be perfectly all right. We expect to get there at low tide, and the boats will leave to come home as soon as the tide starts to rise again.'

Taraivosa's parents agreed and she set off in the crowded boats to go to the reef. When the boats arrived there it was low tide. Taraivosa wandered off by herself. She picked up shells, looked at the brilliantly-coloured fish, stared at her reflection in still pools and had a wonderful time.

Suddenly Taraivosa noticed that where she had been walking on dry reef she was now splashing in water. The tide was coming in fast! She hurried back to where the boats had been left. There was no-one there. Each boat had filled up with people and everyone had thought that Taraivosa was in one of the other boats. They had gone without her.

Taraivosa stood terrified. Slowly the water crept up her legs. She was 20 miles from the village and between her and home lay waters which were full of sharks.

Meanwhile the boats rowed strongly until they got back to Somo-Somo. Taraivosa's father was waiting. He looked in each boat in turn.

'My daughter! Taraivosa. Where is she?' he cried.

At first the people in the boats were confused. Then they realised what had happened. One of the boats turned back straightaway to look for the missing girl.

'There is not much chance that a boat will find her in 20 miles of open sea,' said her father. 'Come my friends, please help me to pray.'

Everyone in the village went with Taraivosa's father and mother to the church. There they prayed together for the safety of the missing girl.

Meanwhile, Taraivosa had decided that rather than wait on the reef to be drowned she might as well start trying to swin back to Gau. Throwing away all her shells she plunged into the water. She put the thought of sharks out of her head and struggled on as hard as she could.

Hour after hour passed. The search boat gave up and returned to the village. Its crew joined the rest of the villagers in their prayers. Taraivosa, with strength she did not know she possessed, kept on swimming.

After almost 24 hours of prayer, Taraivosa's father stood up in the church.

'Friends,' he called out, 'thank you for your help. I am sure our prayers have been worthwhile. I feel that my daughter is nearly home and that I must go down to the beach and light a fire to guide her back.'

So the father and mother went to the little beach of Nukuleka, which means 'Short Sand'. There they built a fire and barbecued some fish.

Taraivosa was almost exhausted. She had lost count of how long she had been in the water. Her arms and legs felt like heavy weights. Just as she thought she could not stay afloat for one minute longer, she saw it. Flickering in the distance were the flames of a fire. A fire meant land – she was nearly home!

Half an hour later the exhausted girl dragged herself out of the water and staggered up the beach towards her overjoyed parents. Feeding her small pieces of fish to give her a little strength, Taraivosa's father and mother then took her home to rest and recover from her ordeal. The whole village rejoiced when they heard the news.

Taraivosa's father said afterwards that he felt his daughter's life had been saved because every single person in the village had prayed. There had been no weak links in the chain that brought her to safety.

The villagers also learned from their mistake. After that, whenever peple went on fishing trips to the reef, they had to travel back in the same boat as the one they had gone out in, so that no-one was left behind.

Hymn

'Father hear the prayer we offer' (*Come and Praise* Vol 1, 48).

Prayer

Dear God, for all those travelling, wherever they may be,
let us remember the words of St. Patrick:

May the strength of God steer us
May the power of God keep us
May the wisdom of God teach us
May the hand of God protect us.
Amen

The Bible says

But where can wisdom be found?
And where is the source of understanding?
No man knows the way to it . . .
Red gold cannot buy it,
nor can its price be weighed out in silver . . .
But God understands the way to it,
he alone knows its source;
for he can see to the ends of the earth
and he surveys everything under heaven.

Job 28: 12–24

Class presentation ideas

Preparation
Set aside one part of the presenting area (by screens, raised staging, etc) as a 'story telling' area, in the form of an office.

If the school has stage lighting, begin with a bright light focused on the story-telling area. Coloured lights can be used as appropriate while the story progresses.

Development
The story-telling area is the 'office' in which Miss Vakatale tells her strange story. Two children play the parts of Miss Vakatale and the author, the rest of the group mime the action as it takes place.

Conclusion
When the dialogue/drama is complete the hymn, prayers and Bible passage could be introduced. To end the assembly a variety of speakers could pose questions for 'further thought':

Speaker 1 Have you noticed how people often co-operate with each other much more in times of real difficulty?

Speaker 2 Have you noticed how a group of people are sometimes much more successful in getting something done than individuals?

Speaker 3 Have you noticed how much we appreciate other people's help when we are worried or in some kind of trouble?

Speaker 4 Have you noticed how much fun it is when a whole class, or school, does something in which everybody plays a part?

Speaker 5 Let us think in silence for one minute about the 'power of prayer'.

9 Saved by a 'borrowed voice'

Presenter's note
Compassion for people with physical handicaps is a regular feature of assemblies, but this story also inspires admiration for a man who surmounted his physical difficulties to save lives.

Introduction
Imagine that you can't listen to your friends' voices, music, the songs of birds or the cheers of a football crowd. Imagine that you cannot speak, sing, shout – or call for help.

This morning's story is about a deaf and dumb man, and a very brave little girl.

Core material
Lavernock Point is near Penarth in South Wales. It is one of those delightful, but dangerous places found round the coast-line of the British Isles. Local people rarely go there because it can only be reached at low tide and it is a very lonely spot. Tourists, however, don't always know this, particularly if they are handicapped in a way which sometimes stops them getting information.

Alan Thomas, Philip and Maureen Reinholdt were all deaf and dumb – and they were in desperate trouble. Along with the Reinholdt's children Sarah and Karen, and seven students, they had been enjoying the beauty of Lavernock Point one May evening. Suddenly, they noticed that the tide had crept in. The water was now very deep – they were trapped. Behind and above towered huge cliffs; sweeping ever nearer was the swirling sea. They had to move – somewhere!

The group scrambled up onto a narrow, rocky ledge and then found they could get no further. Somebody would have to do something. The best climber was Alan Thomas, but if he got to the top how could he summon help quickly enough? He couldn't shout . . . or telephone. It was then that Alan had the idea of taking six-year-old Sarah Reinholdt with him.

Sarah's parents looked at Alan with worried eyes when he indicated what he wanted. They knew that almost certain death faced the group unless desperate measures were taken. They nodded their approval anxiously.

Alan began to climb. On his shoulders, with her arms wrapped tightly round his neck, Sarah clung bravely with all her strength. Inch by inch Alan climbed the sheer cliff face. His arms and legs shook with the strain and sweat poured down his face.

'Come on Alan, come on Alan.' Even though she knew he couldn't hear her Sarah muttered the words aloud. With agonising slowness the little girl and the deaf man got higher and higher.

Suddenly they were at the top! As the exhausted man sank to the ground Sarah shouted for help at the top of her voice. Within minutes somebody out for a walk heard her and raised the alarm.

Soon the coastguards were in action and before long the stranded tourists were being lowered from the ledge into a lifeboat below. Nobody was hurt.

'It was an amazing escape,' said one of the coastguards later. 'That's such a lonely spot nobody goes there. The group would almost certainly have died of exposure. They owe their lives to Alan and Sarah.'

Hymn
'We are climbing' (*Come and Praise* Vol 1, 49)

Prayer
Dear God. Help us to value our voices. Let us use them with joy and pleasure. Give us the wisdom to choose and use words which are encouraging and kind, grateful and sincere. Help us to avoid using words which can hurt and upset.

We need your help please, God.

The Bible says
A word can do more than a gift,
A kind word counts for more than a rich present;
With a generous man you will find both.
                           Ecclesiasticus 18: 16–17

Class presentation ideas

Preparation
Invite volunteers to learn letters from the Deaf and Dumb alphabet, as follows:

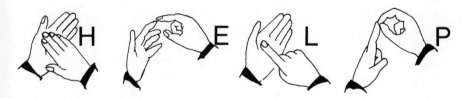

Prepare a series of overhead projector transparencies or picture placards telling the story.

Development
This assembly could be particularly effective if presented in complete silence.
Child presenters spell out H E L P in sign language.
The story is presented on OHP/placards and the group mimes the action.

Follow up
Useful addresses are:
Handicapped Adventure Playground Association, 3 Oakley St, London SW3.
Royal National Institute for the Deaf, 105 Gower St, London WC1E 6AV.
Royal Society for the Prevention of Accidents, Cannon House, The Priory, Queensway, Birmingham B4 6BS.

10 Annie, Bill and Sandy

Presenter's note
This assembly emphasises the need for a 'caring approach' whether it be towards humans or animals.

Introduction
Do you know the saying: 'A dog is man's best friend'? This may be true, but not many people think of dogs as being good actors! This morning's story is about the friendship between a dog and a man, and it is also the story of how this dog became a famous actor. Perhaps he became such a good actor because he knew a lot about the less pleasant things in life. He knew just what it was like to be lonely and unloved.

Core material
The theatre was full and all the people in it were looking forward to seeing the show. It was a very famous one called *Annie*. The curtain went up . . .

The scene was New York in the 1930s and a lonely little girl was wandering the streets. She was running away from an orphanage where she had been cruelly treated. Suddenly she saw another figure in the street – a stray dog, also unloved and unwanted.

'Perhaps I've found a friend at last,' whispered the little girl, Annie. 'I'm going to call you Sandy,' she said as she stroked the poor dog.

The audience was amazed.

'Isn't that dog a marvellous actor,' they said to each other.

'You'd think he really had been lonely and unloved,' said a woman to her husband.

Little did she know how true her words were!

Sandy, the mongrel, was a mixture of Airedale and Irish wolfhound. Although he was a 'star' now he certainly knew all about the other side of life.

Abandoned by several owners the dog had wandered round the north eastern states of America trying to find a new home. Nobody wanted the thin, dirty looking stray and finally he finished up in a dog pound. This is the sort of place where, if an owner is not quickly found for him, a dog is put to sleep.

Most people want a puppy not a full-grown dog. Sandy sat, miserable and neglected, waiting for the end.

It was then that a young man called Bill came to the dog pound. He was a carpenter in the theatre and he had been given the job of finding and training a dog to take part in the new show he was working on – *Annie*.

When Bill saw Sandy he didn't think the dog was really right for the part, but he couldn't forget Sandy's enormous, sad eyes, which told of so much suffering.

'How much is he?' asked Bill.

'Eight dollars,' replied the man in charge of the pound.

'I've only got two with me,' said Bill. 'Can I pay that as a deposit and bring the rest tomorrow?'

'Sorry,' answered the man. 'He's going to be put to sleep in the morning. Its eight dollars now – or that's it.'

Bill hurried back to his lodgings and borrowed six more dollars from the people he worked with in the theatre. Next morning at 6 o'clock he was outside the dog pound, waiting for it to open.

He paid his eight dollars and took Sandy away with him. Together they worked hard for weeks to train Sandy for the show. Then another terrible thing happened. Sandy was run over by a lorry.

This time, however, Sandy had somebody who loved and cared about him. Bill got him to a doctor quickly, and although he was badly hurt, Sandy recovered in time to take his place in the opening of the show.

At first it was only a small show, but eventually it became a tremendous success and Sandy became famous all over the world.

Hymn
'All the animals' (*Come and Praise* Vol 2, 80)

Prayer
Let us think this morning about lonely people and lonely dogs. Let us pray that both can find the happiness which can only be discovered when someone really cares for us.

Amen.

The Bible says
Win your neighbour's confidence when he is poor,
and you will share the joy of his prosperity;
stand by him in time of trouble,
and you will be his partner when he comes into a fortune . . .
Happy is the man who has found a friend.

Ecclestiasticus 22: 23; 25: 9

Class presentation ideas
In this assembly the core material might most appropriately be used towards the end of proceedings, if it is a class or group presentation.

Begin with one of the presenters making a statement:

Speaker 1 'Our assembly this morning has a lot to do with dogs. How many of you have a pet dog? Look . . .'

Children in the class who have dogs as pets put up their hands. (They could be asked in advance to bring in a photograph or painting of their particular pet.) Volunteers could be asked to describe their pet and say how they got their dog. *Speaker 2* reads the introduction, followed by the reading of the story. The latter is too long to be adequately read by most children so a well-rehearsed version might include different children reading the dialogue and descriptive text.

This might lead into the hymn, prayer and Bible reading.

Follow up

The source of this story is a book called *Sandy* (published by Robson books). In this the dog 'tells' his story in his own words. This could lead to interesting follow-up in writing or drama. Another idea for follow up is pet care. Useful material can be obtained from:

Pedigree Petfoods Education Centre, National Office, Waltham-on-the-Wolds, Melton Mowbray, Leicestershire LE14 4RS. Denise Reed, the Education Liaison Officer is most helpful.

11 What weather!

Presenter's note
Newspapers regularly carry stories about the heroism of the rescue services. This material details a busy March night for them.

Introduction
Whenever we set out on a journey – by bus, train, car, ship or aeroplane – we expect to get to our destination safely. Sometimes, however, accidents do happen and, when this is the case, we might need the help of a rescue service. This morning's story is about the brave people who help when there is trouble at sea.

Core material
Monday, March 13th, 1989 was a day of howling gales and raging seas off the coast of Cornwall and the Channel Islands. Aboard the 2000 ton cargo ship *Secil Japan* conditions suddenly changed from unpleasant to dangerous.

'Captain!' cried the First Officer, 'the cargo shifted when that last wave hit us.'

The Greek captain clung desperately to the bridge door as his ship heeled over to a terrifying angle. He knew that the cargo of timber in the hold had moved to one side, making the vessel dangerously unbalanced.

'There's only one thing to do,' shouted the captain to his first officer above the screaming of the wind. 'Send a 'Mayday' signal.'

Soon the international distress signal was crackling over the air waves. As it was picked up at coast guard stations and listening posts immediate action was taken.

'Ship in difficulties off the coast of St Ives,' was the urgent message passed. Within minutes six helicopters, two lifeboats, and shore coast-guard teams were making their way to where the *Secil Japan* was in trouble.

At about 9pm a Sea King helicopter from the Royal Naval Air station at Culdrose reached the ship. As pilot Lt Darrell Nelson hovered overhead he could see the desperate trouble beneath him. Huge 30 ft waves pounded the wheelhouse of the ship as it thrashed ever nearer to the jagged rocks of the coastline.

'It's going to be tricky winching them off,' shouted co-pilot Lt Jim Pollard. As he spoke he pointed to the rock face only 10 yards away from the helicopter as its rotors battled against the fierce winds.

'OK, let's not waste any more time,' replied Darrell Nelson.

Soon the rescue work was under way as the courageous crews of the helicopters and lifeboats went about their life-saving tasks. When the rescue was completed, crews were safely back at base and victims being cared for in hospitals, it was possible to assess the day's work.

The *Secil Japan* had not been the only ship in trouble. One Sea King helicopter had made a 400-mile round trip to airlift an injured seaman from a trawler; 11 Indonesian seamen had been rescued from the *Perintis*, a ship just out from Antwerp which had sunk 30 miles off the German coast.

As the tired crews relaxed they could be certain of one thing – at least 25 seamen would have died but for their skill and bravery.

Hymn
'He's got the whole world in his hands' (*Come and Praise* Vol 1, 19)

Prayer
Dear God, Guard those who must make journeys in dangerous conditions. Give them skill, courage and calmness, when these qualities are most needed.

Let us think also of those brave people of the rescue services; may your strength steer them, your power keep them, your wisdom teach them, your hand protect them.

Amen

The Bible says
Let us now sing the praises of . . . the heroes of our nation's history . . . Their line will endure for all time and their fame will never be blotted out . . . and God's people will sing their praises.

Ecclesiasticus 44: 1, 13–15

Class presentation ideas

Preparation
This could focus on a display including newspaper cuttings on help at disasters; headlines made by the children; amplified tape recordings of 'storms at sea' etc; display/publicity material from organisation such as RNLA.

Development
The whole of the assembly could focus on the people who help when there are accidents and the many organisations involved.

Useful addresses
Royal National Lifeboat Association, West Quay Road, Poole, Dorset B15 1HZ.

Missions to Seamen, St Michael Paternoster Road, College Hill, London EC4R 2RL.

St John's Ambulance Brigade, 1 Grosvenor Crescent, London SW1X 7EF.

Royal Society for the Prevention of Accidents, Cannon House, The Priory, Queensway, Birmingham B4 6BS.

Royal Life Saving Society, 14 Devonshire St, London W1N 2AT.

12 The good old days?

Presenter's note
Children in the past were often much worse off than those of today. Fortunately there were adults who were prepared to do something about this.

Introduction
What might you be having for tea today? What colour is your bedroom? Have you a pet? A bike? A computer? If someone asked you these questions today you probably wouldn't find it difficult to answer. This would not have been the case for many poor children in England's big towns a hundred years ago. Many of them weren't sure what, when, or where they would eat next. Many had no homes, and few could afford luxuries like pets or toys. The 'old days' were only good for some.

Core material
When things aren't going too well, people often talk about 'the good old days'. Between 1850 and 1900 London was in many ways the centre of the world. Trade was booming, industries were growing, new railways were being built, rich businessmen lived in magnificent houses.

But what about the poor people of London? Life was very different for them.

A man whose wife had died was struggling to bring up his sons and find work at the same time. When they missed some time at school he was fined five shillings. He had no money to pay the fine so he was sent to prison for five days. When he came out of prison he found that he and his family had been thrown out of their home. Fearing that he could no longer look after his sons at all he gave them to a travelling circus. One of the boys was displayed in this as 'a living skeleton'.

A visitor to the city wrote in his diary:

'The whole place is alive with street boys, bare-footed, filthy, turning cartwheels for a penny. They swarm on the stairs down to the Thames, stunted, deformed, repulsive.'

There are many other reports about these thousands of poor children – or 'waifs and strays' as they were called – in London at this time. They had no homes and no parents; they never got enough to eat. Many were ill, crippled or deformed because they never had any medical care. Often, they turned to crime in order to survive.

Did anyone care about these desperate children? Yes, and they were determined to help. You may have heard of Dr Barnardo (who founded Dr Barnardo's homes) and General Booth (of the Salvation Army). There was also Marion Bowers, who was herself extremely poor; and Edward de

Montjoie Rudolph, a modest, frail clerk who founded what eventually became the Church of England Children's Society. These were people who cared, and were prepared to do something to help.

Hymn
'Sad, puzzled eyes' (*Come and Praise*, Vol 2, 74)

Prayer
Dear God, let us pray for those children who are still in need. Let us think particularly of those who live in countries where there is a shortage of food, homes, education and health care.

Let us give thanks for those people and organisations who give help, and let us pray for their continued strength and support. Amen

The Bible says
Go out quickly into the streets and alleys of the town and bring me in the poor, the crippled, the blind and the lame.

Luke 14: 21

Class presentation ideas

Preparation
Children involved in the presentation could collect information about the subject in advance – from reference sources and or contacting the organisations listed below.

Development
Divide presenters into two groups:
Group 1 mimes a typical day in the life of a modern child in the UK.
Group 2 mimes the story in the assembly, of the children given away to the circus.
Narrator comments on the caring work of individuals and organisations devoted to helping these children

Conclusion
After this, the point should be made that not *all* children in the UK are well off. Mention could also be made of the plight of millions in the developing world, and what can be done to help them.

Follow up
Facts, figures and opinions related to the subject might be compiled before the assembly. Useful resources for securing these could be: The Church of

England Children's Society, Old Town Hall, Kennington Road, London SE11 4QD.
Dr. Barnardo's Homes, Tanner's Lane, Barkingside, Ilford, Essex.
Salvation Army, National and International HQ., 101 Victoria Street, London EC4.

13 Quick thinking

Presenter's note
This story is one of courage and quick thinking by two schoolboys.

Introduction
You might not expect a journey to school in a school bus to be particularly eventful. Neither did Simon Marsh and Anthony Walters as they set out one September morning. Next morning, though, their photographs were in all the papers – and this is why.

Core material
Anthony Walters took out his handkerchief and blew his nose loudly. He'd hoped that his cold might have got him a day off school, but Mum wasn't taken in.

'If you're well enough to play with your friends at night, you're well enough to go to school,' she'd said. Anthony couldn't argue with that and so he sat, as usual, in the school bus going from his home in Tredegar to Bishop Hadley School in Merthyr Tydfil.

In front of him sat 11-year-old Simon Marsh. Sitting directly behind the driver Simon absent-mindedly watched the man change gear in the heavy traffic. Then, suddenly, he noticed the driver's head drop sideways and lean on the window. For a few seconds he watched transfixed with horror, then . . .

'He's unconscious!' Simon shouted. He leapt out of his seat and grabbed the steering wheel from the driver's lifeless hands. Directing the bus in and out of the heavy traffic he realised that he could not brake to slow it down because the driver's feet were in the way.

Anthony realised that something was desperately wrong. He raced down the bus to help Simon with the large and heavy steering wheel.

'We can't stop it,' shouted Simon.

'No, we'll just have to get away from the traffic. Watch out for a gap on this side of the road.'

'There's one coming up,' gasped Simon, as the bus roared past a long row of terraced houses.

'Right,' nodded Anthony, 'I'm ready.'

'Now!' yelled Simon.

Yanking the steering wheel as hard as they could the two boys slewed the bus off the road. It bumped over the grass verge and they fought to keep it on an even keel. An empty house loomed ahead and with a tremendous crash the bus ploughed into it.

Ten minutes later rescue workers had freed Simon from the wreckage and he was on his way to hospital with a fractured knee. Beside him Anthony nursed a bad gash in his leg.

Both boys were still in hospital the next day when the national newspapers arrived with their photographs on the front pages.

Simon's father, Mr Paul Marsh, spoke for everybody concerned when he said, 'It was a very brave thing that they did. Without their action there could have been a terrible catastrophe'.

Hymn
'Cross over the road' (*Come and Praise* Vol 1, 70)

Prayer
Thank you God for those people who, by their quick thinking and resourceful actions, save others from injury or death.

Amen

The Bible says
Prepare yourself for testing,
Set a straight course, be resolute,
and do not lose your head in time of disaster.
Ecclesiasticus 2: 1–2

Class presentation ideas
Children enjoy hearing about brave acts. The core material of this assembly might be the starting point for a more extensive consideration of different kinds of bravery:

- the sort where unexpected, positive physical action is needed;
- the sort where people deliberately take on a job which requires courage to help others – helicopter pilot/winchman, fire officer, lifeboat crew member etc;
- the bravery needed to withstand personal pain, disappointment, injustice, illness;
- the bravery needed to protest against injustice in situations where doing so seems hopeless.

Such an assembly could draw upon plenty of examples from heroes of the rescue services; stories like that of David Kelly (see Assembly 1); and campaigners like Martin Luther King; through to such Biblical examples as the Good Samaritan (Luke 10: 30–34) and Jesus facing an important Roman (John 19: 8–11).

14 The day he came

Presenter's note
This assembly is really about joy – the anticipation of a new pet's arrival and the sheer joy of the first contact with him.

Introduction
I am sure all of you have really looked forward to something at some time. You will know that feeling of breathless excitement. Listen carefully to the passage which follows.

Core material
We got up really early, Dad and me. It was a spring day in 1943. When we set out to walk there was a sort of mist covering the ground. Our feet disappeared into it and anybody looking at us might have thought we were walking on our knees.

The birds were singing and the hedges were high as we twisted along the narrow road. I could hardly think for excitement and as I put one foot in front of the other I did so in time to the words: 'He's coming . . . He's coming . . . He's coming . . .' which I chanted under my breath.

'What's that?' asked Dad.

'Er . . . where's he coming from, Dad?'

'Aberdeen.'

'On the 7 o'clock train?'

'Right.'

After an hour's walk we stopped. Dad took a medium sized bottle with a screw top out of his pocket and we each had a drink of cold tea.

'Want a mint imperial?' he asked.

'No thanks,' I replied. Why did adults like mints so much?

After another hour we were climbing the steep bank to Durham station. Dad had a word with the gnome-like porter wearing a thick waistcoat with chains across it, and then we sat on a seat on the platform.

The train appeared in the distance like an angry black snake. Smoke puffed up from the engine and it moved in an angry, threatening manner. When it reached the station it hissed its resentment at having to stop and spat and clanked until it came to a reluctant and impatient halt.

'Come on,' said Dad.

We went to the guard's van. The door slid back and a man with thick black hair and a Scottish accent said,

'Ye the party fer this lot?'

'Right,' shouted back my Dad, and took the wicker basket in his arms. He put it down on the seat and we both got down on our hands and knees and looked inside.

A pair of nervous, glittering black eyes looked back at us and a wet nose pushed forward in the hope of a friendly response. Dad scratched him under the chin with a stubby forefinger and was rewarded with a little whine and a bang of the tail on the bottom of the basket.

I could hardly believe it. He was here at last. A pup . . . our dog . . . all the way from Aberdeen.

'I'm going to call him Scottie,' I said.

Hymn
'All the animals' (*Come and Praise* Vol 2, 80)

Prayer
Dear God, Let us pray this morning for pets and owners. We give thanks for the joy, pleasure and companionship which can be given by pets, and we pray that we may always be caring and considerate owners. Let us also say a special prayer for those pets who are neglected or abandoned. May they find somebody to care for them.

Amen

The Bible says
A faithful friend is a secure shelter;
Whoever finds one has found a treasure.
Ecclesiasticus 6:14

Class presentation ideas
This core material might be a starting point for considering feelings such as joy, awe, wonder etc.

The presenters could give individual or group examples of situations and occasions that have caused them to have these feelings. The scope here is vast – pets, weather, sounds, sights, other people. (You may need to focus the discussion on just a few areas.)

15 Prizewinner

Presenter's note

This is an inspiring story of overcoming a severe physical handicap.

Introduction

This morning's story is about a boy who wrote a book. To do so, however, he had to conquer enormous difficulties – as you will hear.

Core material

Learning to type is a bit like learning to do lots of other things – you need to practise. You also need somebody to show you how a typewriter works, and to answer your questions. It helps, too, if your fingers are nimble and can move quickly.

It took Christopher Nolan quite a long time to learn to type. This was not because he didn't practise. He did, but Christopher suffers from a disease called Cerebral Palsy, and he cannot move or speak. He spends his life in a wheelchair.

Despite this, Christopher wanted to write. Even though he couldn't talk he had lots he wanted to say. So he started to learn to type. He did this by having a stick tied to his forehead. He then poked this stick onto the letters of a special typewriter called a Possum.

It was agonisingly hard, slow work but Christoper kept at it, hour after hour. Finally at the age of 15 he finished a book of poems. So many people enjoyed the poems that he was asked to write another book.

So began more hours and hours of work. Some writers dictate their books into a tape recorder and then have them typed up. Others write down their stories in pen or pencil and then have them typed. Obviously Christopher couldn't do either of these things, so it was back to that Possum again.

The book that Christopher wrote this time was called *Under the eye of the clock*. It was so good that it won the Whitbread Book of the Year Award in 1987.

So Christopher became famous for his writing – and tremendously admired for how he had done it.

Hymn

'God knows me' (*Come and Praise* Vol 1, 15)

Prayer

Dear God, Make us grateful for healthy bodies. Give us the understanding to be able to help those who are handicapped in some way. Let the message of Christopher's story be an inspiration to us all.

Amen

The Bible says
Happy the man who has a concern for those
more helpless than himself.

(adapted from Psalm 41:1)

Class presentation ideas

Christopher's story as it is written here could come towards the end of this assembly.

In the introductory part the groups could consider hands and their uses through a mixture of comment and demonstration (tying shoelaces, fingering a recorder, fastening buttons, eating a meal with a knife and fork – and using a typewriter). The aim throughout this activity would be to emphasise how much we use our hands, and how we take so much of this activity for granted.

The second part of the assembly might focus on 'writing stories and poems'. The presenting class might read one or two selections of their favourites and comment on how much effort, time and talent it takes to write an interesting story or poem.

When these two points – of manual dexterity and careful, imaginative thought – have been made, the stage will have been set for the reading of Christopher's moving story.

Further sources

Under the Eye of the Clock by Christopher Nolan, is published by Weidenfeld and Nicolson.

The Spastics Society, 12 Park Crescent, London W1N 4EA.

Unit 4 of the Barnardo's *Primary Education Pack*, available from Tanner's Lane, Barkingside, Ilford, Essex, contains excellent work on this subject.

16 One last try

Presenter's note
The theme of this assembly is determination and persistence – qualities which are sometimes rewarded at the very last moment.

Introduction
Have you ever thought: 'It's not worth it . . . I might as well give up . . . it's no use . . .'?
I think we all have at some time. Today's story is about a man who refused to give up.

Core material
'It's no good,' said the weatherbeaten sea captain. 'After all this time I might as well give up. Nobody's going to listen to me.'

'I'm not sure about that,' replied the serious-looking monk. 'I am not sure at all.'

It was the year 1492. The two men who sat in the quiet courtyard of a monastery at La Rabida, near the port of Palos in Spain were old friends. The monk knew that the sailor had a dream of sailing westwards across the Atlantic Ocean to discover new lands which he was sure were there.

'Seven years,' said the captain, 'seven years I've been trying to raise the money to buy ships to make this voyage. I'm sure there are undiscovered lands out there – but I'll never get to find them now.'

'Well I think its worth one last try,' said the monk. 'Now I know you haven't asked the queen, and when I was a priest I knew her well. Let me write a letter introducing you – and then you can tell her about your dream.'

'I suppose it might be worth one more try,' muttered the captain.

A short time later he was at the palace of King Ferdinand and Queen Isabella of Spain. A courtier showed him into the royal chamber.

'An old friend has told me about you,' said the queen rather haughtily. 'What have you got to say?'

'Your majesty,' began the captain, 'it's like this . . .'

Despite himself the sailor was once more carried away with enthusiasm when he began to speak. He explained that he was sure that there were undiscovered lands, and untold riches, across the cold waters of the Atlantic Ocean. He told of his need for ships and men to make this discovery.

As he talked the queen listened intently. Even the king lost his bored look and stared, fascinated, into the sailor's face.

'When the lands are discovered the whole world will know that it was Spanish ships and men who found them,' the captain said.

'You're right,' said Queen Isabella. 'I will sell some of my jewels to raise money for ships.'

'Agreed,' said the king. 'This is an opportunity which should not be neglected. You must certainly make this expedition. Ships and men must be found. By the way, what did you say your name was?'

The sea captain bowed.

'Thank your majesties. My name is Christopher Columbus.'

Hymn
'The journey of life' (*Come and Praise* Vol 1, 45)

Prayer
Lord, let us think this morning of those who have the courage to explore the unknown.

Let us give thanks for the discoveries which have made our world a fuller and more interesting place.

Please help us in facing the challenge of our own lives, and give us strength to make the right decisions.

Amen

The Bible says
Woe to faint hearts and nerveless hands
and to the sinner who leads a double life!
Woe to the feeble hearted! they have no faith,
and therefore shall go unprotected.
Woe to you who have given up the struggle!
Ecclesiasticus 2: 12–14

Class presentation ideas
Ideas which could be developed include:
- Christopher Columbus set sail on the voyage in which he was to discover America on 17th April, 1492. This core material could be linked with other great voyages of discovery – right up to space travel.
- Compare the qualities needed to be an intrepid explorer with those needed to invent, create and make the various modes of transport which have developed over the years.

17 Ian

Presenter's note
'Making a new start' is the theme of this modern story.

Introduction
We all make mistakes, but sometimes a person seems thoroughly 'bad'. Ian did until something made him think again.

Core material
There are some names which people would not like to be called – thief, vandal, yob, villain. Sadly Ian was all of these. Although just a teenager he had already been in trouble with the police for stealing cars, injuring people and damaging property. Finally he was sent to Borstal. (This is a place where young people who have been in trouble with the police are sent for training which will hopefully make them more law-abiding.)

At Borstal Ian was given the chance to meet different kinds of people. He volunteered to do some work for the disabled and he was sent to a home for the disabled called St George's.

'As soon as I got there it made me think,' said Ian later. 'Here I was, young and fit and causing no end of trouble. Then I saw these quiet, courageous people who were living under terrible handicaps. I felt I just had to give as much help as I possibly could.'

The matron of St George's was so impressed with Ian and his work that she promised him a full-time job as soon as he had done his time in Borstal.

Ian was glad to accept and moved to live as near as he could to his work in the home. Now he is admired and liked by his friends in St George's.

Hymn
'God knows me' (*Come and Praise* Vol 1, 15)

Prayer
> Dear God,
> Help us to change,
> From selfishness to unselfishness,
> From thoughtlessness to thoughtfulness,
> From thinking only of our own needs,
> To thinking about those of others.
> Teach us to be aware of our mistakes,
> And to learn from them.
> Amen

The Bible says

The thief must give up stealing, and instead work hard and honestly with his own hands, so that he may have something to share with the needy.

Ephesians 4: 28

Class presentation ideas

As a preliminary to the narration of this story the presenting class could provide a few thoughts on 'bad' and 'good.' This might be done visually by using colours.

Use two definite colours (*not* black and white). If they are red and yellow some time during the presentation they might be ostentatiously mixed to provide orange – with the obvious connotation that people are rarely extremes, but a mixture of good and bad qualities. Our aim therefore should be to see that the 'good' gets a greater chance to come to the fore.

18   It's never too late to say 'Thank you'

Presenter's note

We hear more about heroes at sea than heroines – this story offers a different perspective. The time factor involved should also provide food for discussion.

Introduction

We don't always say thank you when we should. This morning's story is about a man who had to wait 45 years before he could thank a lady for something she had done for him. It all began on a ship, during the Second World War.

Core material

'She's sinking – we'll be trapped!'

Frantic voices called out as the great ship keeled over and began to sink, only minutes after the enemy torpedo struck.

Below decks Leslie Crossman was in deperate trouble. Trapped in a storage area he found the door leading out of it was jammed.

'Kick it open, Les!' shouted one of the other seamen.

'I can't – it's jammed.'

'Let's kick it together then.'

The men kicked and banged at the door as hard as they could. Suddenly it burst open and Leslie and his friends clambered out quickly. Already the ship was sinking fast, and they had to slide down one of its sides into the water.

Leslie's legs were badly cut and bruised, but he hardly noticed. One thought kept racing through his head:

'I can't swim . . . I can't swim . . . and I had no chance to get a lifejacket.'

Before he could think of anything else Leslie found himself spluttering and gasping in the sea. All round him was chaos and confusion. Boats and rafts bobbed about, people shouted and screamed, but for Leslie there was only one terrifying thought – he didn't know how to stay afloat!

Choking agonisingly as he again sank beneath the surface of the water Leslie suddenly heard a calm voice beside him:

'Don't worry, I've got a lifejacket here for you. It will keep you afloat.'

Then a pair of firm but gentle hands helped Leslie into the lifejacket and he began to float safely on the water. He just had time to see that his rescuer was a young woman before she gave him a smile and swam off strongly to where another ship was picking up survivors. Soon Leslie was picked up by a rescue ship and taken to safety. The rescue happened in June 1942. Years went by, but Leslie never forgot the young lady who had saved his life. He had no idea, however, that he would ever see her again. Much later the *Sunday Express*, newspaper heard about the story and set about searching for the two people involved. After a great deal of effort they were found and a meeting was arranged – but by now the date was 1987 – 45 years later!

When Leslie met the lady who had saved his life his first words were 'Thank you'.

'I've waited a very long time to say that,' said the ex-sailor, with a smile. 'You know – I'm married and I have four children and four grand-children – without you I wouldn't even be alive.'

Audrey Cunningham, the lady who had saved Leslie, nodded her head shyly.

'I'm just glad I was able to help,' she said. 'I learned life saving at school so I knew I could do without my lifejacket.'

'Thank you – again!' replied Leslie.

(adapted from a story in the *Sunday Express*)

Hymn
'Cross over the road' (*Come and Praise* Vol 1, 70)

Prayer
Let us pray this morning for people who work at sea – on fishing boats, liners, cargo ships, weather ships, submarines, oil rigs.
Let us pray that when they are in danger help is nearby.
Amen

The Bible says
'*Let us never tire of doing good, for if we do not slacken our efforts we shall in due time reap our harvest.*
Therefore, as opportunity offers, let us work for the good of all.
Galatians 6: 9–10

Class presentation ideas

Preparation
Set up a display board in a conspicuous place in the assembly area, with several ribbons attached to the centre. Prepare cards entitled: THANK YOU, SWIM, HELP, MEMORY.

Development
The presenting group could use the core material story as the first part of the assembly. After this a narrator could suggest that this story could help our thoughts go in several directions. *Presenter 1* takes one ribbon and fixes the card saying THANK YOU to the end. This could be followed by comment on when we should say thank you in everyday life, for what, how often we forget, and so on.

The second ribbon/card/comment could be on self-preservation, the need to keep fit, learn to swim etc. The third could be on our readiness, willingness, capability to help when called upon – in a wide variety of situations. The fourth ribbon/card/comment could be used to remind us to stay constant and not forget old friends, people who have helped us in the past etc.

19 City Story

Presenter's note
One of the most heartening aspects of this story of modern, urban difficulties is that its end is the beginning of hope for others.

Introduction
It is hard to think of helping people who sometimes behave in a way which embarrasses, or even frightens, us. This story about a young lady and one of London's homeless tramps makes us think about this situation.

Core material
To get to the place where she worked Sue had to travel to Oxford Circus underground station in London. Each day as she came out of the station she noticed a sad sight.

A group of men regularly sat on the pavement there. They were very dirty and their clothes were in rags. They spent their days and nights sleeping on the pavement and they begged from passers-by.

'Good morning.'

Sue made a point of speaking each morning, and sometimes stopped for a longer chat with the men.

'If only I could do more to help,' she thought to herself. Then she began to bring them food several times a week, and when the weather got colder she bought them all a new pair of socks. The men got to know Sue and looked forward to her visits.

Time passed by and Sue had a few days holidays. When she returned to work she was shocked to find that one of her friends from outside the station had been taken to hospital. She found out which hospital he was in and went to visit him.

'How is he?' she asked a doctor after the visit.

'Well, not very good I'm afraid,' replied the doctor. 'He has neglected his health for far too long. We are going to have to remove one of his legs.'

After his operation Sue continued to visit the unfortunate man as often as she could. She took him small presents, spent a long time talking to him and, as she had been a nurse, helped and encouraged him as much as possible. He appeared to be making good progress.

When she arrived at the hospital one day, his bed was empty. She knew from the sad faces of the nurses that it was bad news. Her friend had died during the night.

Sue left sadly but a few days later she received a telephone call asking her to go back to the hospital. When she got there she was told that her friend had left a ragged bundle with her name on it. When Sue opened the dirty clothes she found, to everybody's surprise, a wad of bank notes. All together there was £200, and a little note thanking Sue for all her kindness.

For a moment Sue felt too upset to say anything. Later, she gave £100 of the money to a hospital for sick children, and she gave the rest to help people in countries which are much poorer than England.

Hymn
'Lord of all hopefulness' (*Come and Praise* Vol 1, 52)

Prayer
> Dear God,
> Give me love in my heart,
> keep me serving.
> Give me love in my heart I pray.
> Give me love in my heart, keep me serving.
> Keep me serving till the break of day.
>
> (adapted from a traditional hymn)

The Bible says
When you helped the least of my brothers you helped me.
adapted from Matthew 25: 40

Class presentation ideas
This story lends itself to development of a number of themes: helping others, inner city problems, judging by appearances . . .

Some schools have links with particular helping agencies, national or local. One such project is St Botolph's Day Centre. My school raises funds for the Centre and sends its harvest produce there.

For more information contact: St Botolph's Day Centre, Aldgate, London EC3N 1AB.

20 The Hero

Presenter's note
This story of a mid-air collision emphasises the greatest sacrifice of all – giving up one's life for another.

Introduction
This morning's story is of a very brave man. He was the pilot of a RAF plane which took off one morning from an airfield in Yorkshire.

Core material
'This is going to be great!'

Cadet Derek Coates looked at the propellers turning on the Welington bomber and thought to himself again.

'In a few minutes I'll be in the air.'

Teenager Derek was a member of the Middlesborough Air Training Corps. He was being given some flying experience at RAF Station Leeming.

Slowly the old bomber trundled down the runway and, with the skilled hands of Flight Lieutenant Alan Quinton at the controls, it began its gradual climb into the air.

The excited Derek stood beside the pilot as the plane settled on course. Suddenly, and apparently out of nowhere, another plane appeared and with a terrifying, nerve tearing crash, the two aircraft collided.

Fighting with the controls of the damaged plane Flt. Lt. Quinton knew that it was badly damaged. He seized the only parachute in the cockpit and, speaking as quickly and carefully as he could, he told Derek how to put it on and use it.

'Good luck,' whispered the brave pilot. The great plane gave another sudden lunge and Derek found himself falling through mid-air.

Although he had never had a parachute on in his life before Derek landed safely. Sadly both of the planes involved in the collision crashed, killing everyone else on board.

When he had recovered from his ordeal, Derek told of Flt Lt Quinton's calm, selfless bravery, which had undoubtedly save his life. The brave pilot was posthumously awarded the George Cross.

Hymn
'He who would valiant be' (*Come and Praise* Vol 1, 44)

Prayer
Dear God,
Let this morning's story act as an inspiration to us.

Help us to be aware of the qualities of so many people in
the world.
Make us worthy of you and them.
Amen

The Bible says
There is no greater love than this, that a man should lay down his life for his
friends.

John 15:13

Class presentation ideas
One way in which to approach this serious and inspiring assembly in terms of a
class presentation might simply be to have the story read by a selection of
readers. To highlight the effect a series of staging blocks could be positioned in
the staging area.

As each presenter reads his or her part of the story they could step up onto
the block, stepping down again immediately afterwards.

Supplementing this might be a display of Air Training Corps information.
This is still a flourishing organisation in many areas. The assembly might be
ended by the reading of the Bible passage given here.

21 An unusual man

Presenter's note
Some lesser-known facts about Albert Schweitzer are as inspiring as his more famous deeds.

Introduction
This morning we are going to hear about a famous man called Albert Schweitzer. He was famous for several things – but we are going to learn about some of his less well-known acts.

Core material
Albert Schweitzer was possibly one of the most famous men of the twentieth century. A brilliant scholar, a wonderful musician, he gave up the possibility of a profitable career in Europe to go to a disease-ridden part of Africa and set up a hospital there.

His work at the hospital made him world-famous and in 1952 he received the Nobel Peace Prize. Despite his great achievements however, some of the smaller things in his life can perhaps help us to understand what an exceptional person he was. Here are three of them.

1   When Albert was a small boy in Europe he went to a village school. He was well off and well dressed, but many of the other children weren't. He decided to put this right in the best way he could so he took his best clothes to school with him and gave them away to the other children.
2   Much later a visitor was amazed at all the Africans who were wandering in and around Schweitzer's hospital at Lambarene.
    'Surely all these people aren't ill?' queried the visitor. 'They are walking round and they look perfectly well.'
    'Oh they are,' said Albert Schweitzer, 'but you see those who are ill get very worried and afraid when they have to go to hospital so I always let patients bring one or two of their relatives along to cook for them and keep them company.'
3   Finally some building work was going on at the hospital, but Albert suddenly stopped it and directed the workmen to build in another spot.
    'I wonder why?' Said one of the workmen.
    'Ah,' replied another. 'I know. If we had gone on building there we would have damaged an ants' nest.'

Hymn
'The best gift' (*Come and Praise* Vol 1, 59)

Prayer

Dear God, Help us to value small acts of kindness as well as large ones. Teach us to give how and where we can, in the best ways we can. Help us to remember that we can give time, effort and talents. May we learn from the example of people like Albert Schweitzer.

Amen

The Bible says

The memory of him will not die but will live on from generation to generation;
the nations will talk of his wisdom,
and his praises will be sung in the assembly.
If he lives long, he will leave a name in a thousand,
and if he goes to his rest his reputation is secure.

Ecclesiasticus 39: 9-11

Class presentation ideas

Preparation

This could take the form of a 'question and answer' routine, with a question master and a group who are getting to respond to the questioning.

Development

Begin the session as follows:

Question master   What is the last kind deed you can remember?

Presenter 1   Well, it was last week. My friend . . .

This could then lead on to the core material, which could reinforce the idea of the importance of 'small' kindnesses. Alternatively, incidents described in the core material could be dramatised.

Follow up

Children might be interested in finding out more about Albert Schweitzer. A helpful source is the *Oxford Junior Encyclopaedia* – Vol 5 'Great Lives'.

22 I wonder

Presenter's note
Mystery, awe and wonder are essential ingredients of Religious Education. The following passage, written by a child, focuses on these things.

Introduction
The world is full of things that we wonder about. It is full of mysteries and unanswered questions too. What sort of things puzzle you? Listen carefully to the following words written by a young girl. Perhaps you have similar thoughts to her . . .

Core material
I've got a name and an address and I know how old I am. I've got a brother and a sister and a mum and dad and we've got two cats as pets.

I know that I like chocolate, PE, Spring weather and music. I don't like maths, going to bed early, football on TV, sitting down for a long time.

I know that my hair is brown, my eyes are blue, I'm tall for my age and I've had two abscesses on my teeth.

But what about what I think? Do other people have the same thoughts as me? Do they think why, what, when, where? Why am I here? Why is the sky blue? Why can't we see in the dark?

What is going on in the house with the frilly curtains? What makes our headmaster speak very quietly when he is very angry? What makes daffodils look like yellow trumpets?

When will I feel 'grown up'? When will I stop looking like a beanpole? When will I need to wear glasses?

Where do clouds drift across the sky to? Where do feelings go – happy, sad, worried – why aren't we the same all the time? Where does time go?

Does anybody else wonder as much as I do?

(Susan, aged 11)

Hymn
'The Pilgrim's Hymn' (*Come and Praise* Vol 2, 146)

Prayer
>Dear God,
>Help us to value
>Our talents
>Our imagination
>Our hopes

Our dreams.
Dear God,
Give us strength to cope with
Our fears
Our worries
Our loneliness
Our disappointments.
Dear God,
Increase our awareness
Of ourselves
And of
The world around us.
Amen

The Bible says
Put away anxious thoughts about food to keep you alive and clothes to cover
your body. Life is more than food, the body more than clothes.

Luke 12: 22–23

Class presentation ideas
After reading the passage, the presenters might suggest further individual thoughts. The emphasis could then move from the individual to the group . . . How pleasant and exciting it is to share experiences of wonder and awe; how reassuring it is to share worries and doubts and know that others feel as we do.

As a conclusion, the presenters could point out that while each of us is unique, none of us is alone. Together, therefore, we can appreciate the mystery and wonder of the world in a much more fulfilling way.

23 Got a friend?

Presenter's note
This assembly deals with a subject of paramount importance to primary school children – friendship.

Introduction
I expect most of you are standing (or sitting) beside a friend at this moment. Just turn and look at this friend. You can see eyes, hair, nose, mouth – but you can't see those qualities which make him, or her, your friend. You know about them though. Now listen to this poem.

Core material
> Got a friend?
> I have.
> If I'm hungry or thirsty
> I know he'll share.
> If I'm lonely or ill
> I know he'll care.
> When I'm happy and ready to laugh
> He's glad.
> When I'm miserable and want to cry
> He's sad.
> If I say thoughtless things
> He'll forgive me.
> If I try something new
> He'll support me.
> Got a friend?
> I have.
>
> Geoffrey Simpson

Hymn
'I was lying in the roadway' (*Come and Praise* Vol 2, 88)

Prayer
> Let us pray this morning for friendship in our school.
> May we live happily and joyfully with each other.
> Let there be care and concern in all our friendships.
> Let us remember that a school is only as good as the people in it.
> Dear God, help us to make our school a place where people

Feel welcome, content and secure.
Amen

The Bible says
A faithful friend is a secure shelter;
Whoever finds one has found a treasure.
A faithful friend is beyond price;
He is worth more than money can buy.
                    Ecclesiasticus 6: 14–15

Class presentation ideas
Following the normal greeting one of the presenters could open proceedings
with a statement like the following:

Presenter 1   A dozen is another way of saying 12 – but a 'Baker's
                 dozen' means 13. I wonder how this came about?
Presenter 2   I know.
Presenter 1   Would you tell the rest of us?
Presenter 2   During the reign of King John, bread was the most
                 important food in most people's lives. If bakers in
                 London sold bread which was underweight they were
                 likely to be severely punished. So to make sure they were
                 never guilty of this they made 13 loaves to be sold for the
                 price of 12 – a 'Baker's dozen'.
Presenter 1   So they made more than they needed to?
Presenter 2   Yes.

This point could then be developed in the rest of the assembly. The idea of
giving more than we need or going the second mile (see Matthew 5: 40 'and if
anyone would sue you and take your coat, let him have your cloak as well; and
if anyone forces you to go one mile, go with him two miles . . .') could
eventually lead to the fact that this is what friendship is all about. When this
stage has been reached the 'core material' could be used to conclude the
assembly.

24 Rome: 269

Presenter's note
The core material for this assembly focuses attention on people's need for love and care.

Introduction
One of the dictionary definitions of the word 'love' is: 'warm affection which delights'. Love also means caring for people, no matter what the danger or cost, and being prepared to forgive them. This morning's story is about a famous saint whose name will always be linked with love and care.

Core material
I expect you've all heard of Saint Valentine. On Valentine's Day (February 14th) people exchange cards with poems and messages, eg

> 'Please make me happy.
> Make me feel FINE.
> Please say you'll be
> My VALENTINE.'

Who was St Valentine?

The small group of men in the cave shivered with fear. They were hungry, cold and very frightened.

'What's to become of us?'

'The priest said he would keep us safe.'

'But can we trust him?'

It was the year 269. The hiding men were all Christians. Outside, in the city of Rome, the soldiers of the Emperor Claudius were rounding up Christians. The Emperor had given a firm order – Christianity must be stamped out for ever. However this was not easy to achieve. Many Christians were brave people who would not give up their religion. And so, all over the city, known Christians were hiding until it was safe again.

One of the men who was doing his best to help was a priest called Valentine. He found safe places for Christians to hide, and got food for them.

'There's somebody coming,' whispered one of the men in the cave.

'It must be Valentine.'

'No, there are two of them.'

'It's a Roman soldier! We've been betrayed!'

Valentine was now near enough to the cave to hear the panic-stricken whispers. He called out.

'My friends, don't worry. There's nothing to worry about.'

Minutes later he was introducing the Roman soldier. He was a Christian and had asked Valentine if he would take his wedding service. Although this was very dangerous for both of them, Valentine agreed.

The weeks passed by. By now, however, Valentine was a suspect. The Romans had been watching him for some time. Early one morning he was arrested. He made no attempt to deny that he was a Christian who had been helping other Christians. Because of this he was sentenced to death and thrown into prison to await execution.

In prison Valentine was at first cruelly treated by the jailor, who was often helped by his blind daughter. Whatever happened to him, however, the priest was always polite, kind and gentle to the blind girl. The jailor began to see what being a Christian meant.

By the time the date was fixed for Valentine's execution, the jailor had come to admire him very much, and so had his daughter.

We don't really know how this story ended. We do know that Valentine was put to death, but one story says that he cured the girl's blindness before this happened. Another says that he left her a card signed with his name – perhaps this is where the tradition of Valentine's cards began?

We know, too, that neither Claudius nor anybody else was able to stop the growth of Christianity.

Class presentation ideas

The core material here could be used to initiate another story which reinforces the theme. Two speakers might start things off by saying:

Speaker 1   We have seen that love is giving and forgiving, and being loyal and caring.

Speaker 2   We know another good story to show these qualities.

Introduce the story of Odysseus and Penelope. This could be presented in one of several ways:

- told by the teacher herself, accompanied by 'sound effects' from a chorus of presenters
- told by several children, in narrative form
- as a spoken play, with different children reading each character's part
- read in advance and recorded on tape, then replayed during the assembly, while group members mime the 'action'.

Odysseus, King of Ithaca, had to leave his kingdom at the beginning of the Trojan wars. These lasted for ten years. When they were finished he set sail for home, his kingdom, and his wife Penelope.

No sooner had he begun this journey than Odysseus ran into one terrible adventure and disaster after another. Ten more years passed as he struggled to make his way home.

Meanwhile Penelope was having a dreadful time too. She loved Odysseus and was sure he would return to her. But everyone else told her that he must be dead, and over a hundred men asked to marry her. They moved into her palace, ate her food, argued amongst themselves, and made her life miserable.

Penelope used all sorts of tricks to try and avoid trouble which her refusal to marry seemed to be causing. She started to weave a great robe and told all her suitors that she would decide which one of them she would marry when she had finished it. Then, every night, she secretly undid the work she had done during the day. After four years, however, the suitors began to grow suspicious.

But in another part of the kingdom other events were taking place. Unknown and unrecognised by anyone Odysseus had at last succeeded in getting back. He soon heard the stories of the men at the palace and he knew that unless he was very careful they would kill him for getting in the way of their plans.

Disguising himself as an old beggar, he sought out his son, Telemachus. Telemachus was overwhelmed with delight at seeing his father safe and sound again – and the two men worked out a plan.

A few days later the 'old beggar' arrived at the palace. When he asked to see the queen all the suitors came out to ridicule him and sent him away in a flurry of blows. Penelope was horrified at their cruelty, but really it was all part of the plan. Whilst the 'beggar' was causing all this fuss, Telemachus and some of his friends were collecting up all the suitors' weapons from the armoury.

So it came to the evening. The 'beggar' was gone and Penelope could hold out no longer. She agreed that the first person to bend the great bow which had hung on the wall since Odysseus' departure, would marry her.

One after the other tried. After 50 unsuccessful attempts Penelope was so upset at seeing her husband's bow treated in this way that she went to her room. Shortly afterwards Odysseus burst into the great room, seized the bow and bent it to the full.

His enemies then realised who he was and thought this the perfect opportunity to make sure he was dead. They rushed to the armoury for their weapons only to find that Telemachus and his friends were waiting for them. The intruders were driven from the palace for ever.

Odysseus then got rid of his disguise and sent an old nurse to bring his wife. Unable to believe her eyes Penelope saw that her husband had returned. With tears of joy and relief this loyal and loving wife was at last re-united with her husband.

25 The park

Presenter's note

The Biblical quotation attached to this assembly is: 'Glory to God in the Highest; and on earth peace among men.'

These words are most familiar in a Christmas context, but they seem equally appropriate to this observation of a park throughout the year.

Introduction

Think of a park you know. Can you imagine what it looks like at his moment?

Can you imagine what it would feel like to be in it?

Can you think of that park at other seasons of the year? Think about this for a few seconds, and then listen to this reading.

Core material

The park is near where I live, I walk through it every day on my way to school. Once I turn off the busy main street and walk through the entrance gates it is like another world.

In autumn the red and gold leaves crinkle crisply under my feet and wood smoke from bonfires spirals tentatively up into the sky. People walk along the paths briskly and dogs enjoy extra fun snuffling in the leaves.

When winter comes the park changes. Its outline is clearer and harsher, framed by the skeletons of bare trees silhouetted against a hard, blue sky. The paths are brittle and slippery. There are fewer people now, and those who are about brace their shoulders and breathe deeply, sending tiny clouds in advance of their fast pace.

Spring seems to come with an unexpected rush. Flashes of colour pierce the soil near the rockery on the corner as the first flowers rise bravely into view. Soon the sweep of green in the park's centre is decorated with bunches of swaying, yellow-headed daffodils. There seems to be more laughter from the humans, and an extra bounce in the dogs.

Finally it is summer. The air is heavy with warmth and the sound of insects. Great banks of flowers splash colours in all directions and the trees are thick and green. In the shade beneath them mums play with tiny babies as push chairs are parked in pairs. Everything seems to move slowly as if to say, 'Let's enjoy *this* day'.

Hymn

'Lay my white cloak' (*Come and Praise* Vol 2, 112)

Prayer

'Lord help us to remember that

We are children of the universe,
No less than the trees and the stars.
Help us to be careful and happy,
Because, despite its disappointments,
It is still a beautiful world.'

(adapted from a prayer of 1692)

The Bible says
Glory to God in the Highest, and on earth peace among men.

Luke 2:14

Class presentation ideas

This passage has the great advantage of being appropriate for any time of the year, because each of the seasons is featured in it.

A class assembly might consider the seasons in greater depth or make the link between these seasons and the seasons of the Christian year. The following quotations might be useful in thinking about the seasons.

Spring, the sweet spring is the year's pleasant king;
Then blooms each thing, then maids dance in a ring,
Cold doth not sting, the pretty birds do sing.

(Thomas Nashe)

Here we come a piping
In spring-time and in May;
Green fruit a ripening,
And winter fled away.

When daisies pied, and violets blue,
And ladysmocks all silver white,
And cuckoo buds of yellow hue
Do paint the meadows with delight.

(Shakespeare)

How beautiful is the rain!
After the dust and heat,
In the broad and fiery street,
In the narrow lane,
How beautiful is the rain.

(from: *Rain in Summer* by Longfellow)

The red rose and the lily fair,
That charm our summer day –
There's not a lady in the land
So finely dressed as they.

The autumn is an old friend
That pleases all he can,
And brings the bearded barley
To glad the heart of man.

The mellow year is hasting to its close;
The little birds have almost sung their last,
Their small notes twitter in the dreary blast.

(Coleridge)

Walk fast in snow, in frost walk slow,
And still as you go, tread on your toe;
When frost and snow are both together,
Sit by the fire and spare shoe leather.

26 The Sailor

Presenter's note
So often we make the mistake of judging people by their appearances – as this poem shows.

Introduction
Horatio Nelson was one of Britain's greatest heroes. A statue of this great and brave sailor stands high over London's Trafalgar Square. The following poem about him is however, a very unusual one. Listen to it carefully.

Core material

> The man was small
> So small
> As to look like a boy.
> Not strong at all.
> One eye was covered by a patch
> One arm just an empty sleeve.
>
> 'He's not much to look at
> Is he?
> No, a proper weed.
> Can't see well
> Looks like he'd be useless
> At just about everything.'
>
> 'What's his name?'
> 'Horatio Nelson.'
> 'Horatio Nelson?
> You mean.......
> Horatio Nelson!
>
> He's got hidden strength
> Hasn't he?
> A shrewd, knowing eye.
> The way he looks,
> You can tell he's a man
> Of courage and action.'

John Spink

Hymn
'I come like a beggar' (*Come and Praise* Vol 2, 90)

Prayer

Dear God, help us to remember that none of us has any choice about how we look. Teach us to value people, not for what they look like, but for what they *are* like.

Amen

The Bible says

Do not overrate one man for his good looks or be
repelled by another man's appearance.
The bee is small among the winged creatures,
yet her perfume takes first place for sweetness.

Ecclesiasticus 11: 2–3

Class presentation ideas

Preparation

Three ideas for introducing this assembly are:

● a reading of a well-known Aesop fable – The Tortoise and the Hare. In the story, the arrogant Hare challenges the other animals to a race. He is contemptuous when the Tortoise takes up the challenge. When the race starts the Hare is so confident that he takes a rest – and falls asleep. The Tortoise meanwhile plods on, passes his sleeping opponent and wins the race. Moral: 'Don't judge by appearances.

● play a short piece of music by Beethoven.

● prepare a mime of the story of the Good Samaritan.

Development

Depending on which opening is used, the presenters could draw out the theme of 'not judging by appearances' as follows:

● After highlighting the moral of the Aesop strory, the presenter could point out that Aesop himself had an ugly, misshapen body, but a wonderful mind.

● After the Beethoven passage – Beethoven was deaf and often bad-tempered, yet he created beautiful music.

● After the Good Samaritan mime – of all the people who passed the injured man, the Good Samaritan *seemed* the most unlikely one to help him, because he came from an enemy race. But he showed the most kindness and love.

27 The life of a child

Presenter's note
This fictional passage reminds us that children were cruelly exploited in this country comparatively recently.

Introduction
Imagine if, instead of coming to school this morning, you had been sent out on a job which terrified you. You did this job every day of the week – and were probably beaten by your master every day as well.

Try and compare your life with Tom's as you listen to this passage.

Core material
Once upon a time there was a little chimney sweep, and his name was Tom. That is a short name, and you have heard it before, so you will not have much trouble in remembering it. He lived in a great town in the North Country, where there were plenty of chimneys to sweep, and plenty of money for Tom to earn and his master to spend. He could not read nor write, and did not care to do either; and he never washed himself, for there was no water up the court where he lived. He had never been taught to say his prayers. He never had heard of God, or of Christ, except in words which you never have heard, and which it would have been well if he had never heard. He cried half his time, and laughed the other half. He cried when he had to climb the dark flues, rubbing his poor knees and elbows raw; and when the soot got into his eyes, which it did every day of the week; and when his master beat him which he did every day of the week; and when he had not enough to eat, which happened every day of the week likewise.

(From: *The Water Babies* by Charles Kingsley)

Hymn
'Sad puzzled eyes' (*Come and Praise* Vol 2, 74)

Prayer
Let us think this morning about some words which come from the American Constitution:

'All men are created equal; they are endowed by their Creator with certain unalienable rights; among these are life, liberty, and the pursuit of happiness.'

The Bible says
Let the children come to me; do not try to stop them; for the Kingdom of God

*belongs to such as these. I tell you, whoever does not accept the Kingdom of
God like a child will never enter it.*

Mark 10: 14–15

Class presentation ideas

Preparation
Prepare two 'interview' areas. Put a placard on each, designating them as
'NOW' and 'THEN'. Make both easily visible to the audience.

Development
The whole theme of this assembly is to compare and contrast. Two
interviewers should be chosen from the presenters, they will control
proceedings in each interviewing area.

Interviewer 1 asks a group of children from NOW – about their homes,
food, spare time, hobbies, holidays, school etc.

Interviewer 2 interviews a group of children from THEN who work as
chimney sweeps, or in mills and mines. Their questions would be more
concerned with work, lack of hygiene, inadequate food and sleep, brutality.
The questioning should switch from group to group regularly so that the
contrasts are highlighted.

Conclusion
The supplements used for this assembly could be added to by using material
which the presenting children themselves have devised and written during the
preparation of the assembly.

28 About Ben Adhem

Presenter's note
This short poem makes the point of 'Love thy neighbour' very succinctly.

Introduction
Today's poem may make us think about something which is important in our school, our street, our village, our town. Listen carefully.

Core material

Aban Ben Adhem (may his tribe increase!)
Awoke one night from a deep dream of peace.
And saw, within the moonlight in his room,
Making it rich, and like a lily in bloom,
An angel writing in a book of gold:
Exceeding peace had made Ben Adhem bold,
And to the presence in the room he said,
'What writest thou?' – The vision rais'd its head,
And with a look made all of sweet accord,
Answer'd, 'The names of those that love the Lord.'
'And is mine one?' said Abou. 'Nay not so,'
Replied the angel. Abou spoke more low,
But cheerly still; and said, 'I pray thee, then,
Write me as one that loves his fellow men.'
The angel wrote, and vanished. The next night
It came again with a great awakening light,
And show'd the names whom love of God had blest,
And lo! Ben Adhem's name led all the rest.

Leigh Hunt

Hymn
'When I needed a neighbour' (*Come and Praise* Vol 1, 65)

Prayer
Please God, help us to have the qualities of a good neighbour. Show us how to be kind, reliable, helpful and sincere. Teach us also to be cheerful and to know the value of a smile.

The Bible says
Love thy neighbour as thyself.

Matthew 22:39

Class presentation ideas

This poem could initiate an assembly which takes a closer look at 'Love thy neighbour' and examines some of the qualities needed to do this.

Drama plus narration might be good mediums to convey this theme and it can be shown in slightly different contexts by stories such as:

Joseph forgiving his brothers (Genesis 50: 15–21. see also Assembly 52)

David forgiving Saul (1 Samuel 24: 1–12)

Jesus befriending Zacchaeus (Luke 19: 1–10)

The many people who are described in *The Faith in Action* Series, published by Religious Education Press.

The work of organisations such as Shelter, Christian Aid, Oxfam

Added to these sources, newspapers often have 'good neighbour' stories in them. Children could be encouraged to collect and display such items.

29 Maths gone wrong

Presenter's note

The poem which follows was inspired by statistics from Save the Children on world food figures. The 'slices of bread' are symbolic but convey the point very practically to children (see also presentation ideas).

Introduction

This morning we are going to think about people who have less than us – and just how much less.

Core material

> Think of a sum to show
> Bread and people.
> How much of one
>   for
> How many of the other.
> For the South American
> It's one slice per person.
> Fair enough. For the Middle East too.
> In Africa, half is the ration.
> Two people, one slice.
> In Europe and Russia
> And the States
> There's more than plenty.
> For every five
> There's twelve slices of bread.
> But what about Asia?
> Not even half for every eleven.
> There's just
> One
> Two
> Three
> Four
> Five
> Slices of bread.
>
> Geoffrey Simpson

Hymn

'In Christ there is no East or West' (*Come and Praise* Vol 1, 66)

Prayer

Probably nobody does more for deprived people than Mother Teresa. It might therefore be appropriate here to use the 'Prayer for Peace' which she first introduced in 1981:

> Lead me from Death to Life; from Falsehood to Truth.
> Lead me from Despair to Hope; from Fear to Trust.
> Lead me from Hate to Love; from War to Peace.
> Let Peace fill our Hearts, our World, our Universe.
> Peace, Peace, Peace.

The Bible says

Do not cheat a poor man . . . or keep him waiting with hungry eyes. Do not tantalize a starving man or drive him to desperation in his need . . . When a poor man speaks to you, give him your attention and answer his greeting politely.

Ecclestiasticus 4: 1–8

Class presentation ideas

There are several which could be effective here. One is to have a loaf of sliced bread for sharing out as the poem is being read. This works very well and evokes instant attention.

Ask children to get into five groups – one for each area mentioned in the poem. Share out a loaf of bread in the way described, while the poem is being read.

This could be followed up by a harvest festival service if the time of year is right. If not then it could lead on to more details about 3rd World deprivation and what we can do to help.

Another possibility is to look at 'sharing' closer to home. What talents can we share to enhance the lives of others – a cheerful smile, a good singing voice, a willingness to do jobs that others don't want to do etc?

30 After the storm

Presenter's note
Today's poem could be used to introduce several themes – beauty, seasons, the world around us. In this instance, however, the follow-up work is mainly concerned with water.

Introduction
Today's assembly begins with a poem. As you listen, try and see, in your mind's eye, all the things that are happening.

Core material

> There was a roaring in the wind all night;
> The rain came heavily and fell in floods;
> But now the sun is rising calm and bright;
> The birds are singing in the distant woods;
> Over his own sweet voice the Stock-dove broods;
> The Jay makes answer as the Magpie chatters;
> And all the air is filled with the pleasant noise of waters.
>
> All things that love the sun are out of doors;
> The sky rejoices in the morning's birth;
> The grass is bright with rain drops; – on the moors
> The hare is running races in her mirth;
> And with her feet she from the plashy earth
> Raises a mist: that, glittering in the sun,
> Runs with her all the way, wherever she doth run.
>
> William Wordsworth

Hymn
'It's the springs' (*Come and Praise* Vol 2, 82)

Prayer

> O Lord,
> Thank you for giving us water to drink.
> Thank you for giving us water so that fruit and crops will grow.
> Thank you for giving us water to have so much fun in on holiday.
> Help us to remember those people who suffer because they have not got enough water.
> Amen

The Bible says
Men shall live in peace of mind on the open pastures and sleep in the woods. I will settle them in the neighbourhood of my hill and send them rain in due season, blessed rain.

Ezekiel 34: 26–27 (adapted)

Class presentation ideas
The core material could be the introduction to an assembly which has 'water' as its theme. The presenters might split up into groups and each could consider a specific aspect of the theme, eg:

Group 1 might consider everyday use of water in the British Isles – drinking, washing, cooking, watering gardens, plants, swimming; problems when water freezes.

Group 2 might consider countries where water still has to be drawn from wells and carried; impure water which must always be boiled, irrigation needs.

Group 3 might consider the power of water – dams, electricity, the sea, the life-giving qualities of the oasis.

Group 4 might provide musical links with water. A wide variety is available from Handel's *Water Music* through Debussy's *La Mer* to *Singing in the Rain*.

Group 5 might consider water in the Bible, where it features strongly: scarcity makes it valuable (Psalm 23:2); water carriers from wells (John 4: 5–7); how water had to be bought (Numbers 20:19); how a fountain symbolises God's gift of water (Revelation 21:6).

Group 6 might present a combination of poems and pictures involving water.

31 It's your fault

Presenter's note
As all primary teachers know, children of this age-group hate to be thought 'different' in a context which might lead to being bullied, ostracised, victimised etc. This assembly invokes comparison and understanding for those who may be considered 'different' in any way.

Introduction
None of us likes to be treated unfairly. Try and imagine what it must have been like to have been Ivor in the passage which follows. Evacuees were children who were sent away from their own homes during the Second World War to parts of the country which were thought to be safe from air raids.

Core material
The gang all lived in a long street of terraced houses. Out the front was the main road but at the back there was a large stretch of cornfields, bordered by blackberry-crammed hedges in autumn. The lane between the back of the houses and the fields was the gang's Wembley football stadium in the winter and Lords cricket ground in the summer.

There were three boys in the gang, John, Jim and Brian – that is until the day in 1940 when the evacuee arrived. He was called Ivor and he came from London. He moved into the end house with Mrs Craggs. He didn't know anything about Sunderland or Newcastle players – and he wasn't interested in football!

Ivor hadn't been in the village long when the air raids started.

They were usually on the docks on the coast but the boys were got up by their parents every night and taken to the air raid shelters 'just in case'. Extra brick shelters were built in the lane, sweets and ice cream disappeared from the shops, dads began to disappear and mums got more and more tetchy.

'It's all your fault,' said John one day, as the gang walked to school, with Ivor tagging along behind.

'How do you mean?' asked Ivor nervously.

'Well – it is isn't it? They've built those rotten shelters where we played football, and there's no sweets anymore is there? It wasn't like that before you came!'

'But . . .'

'Yeah,' Jim and Brian joined in. 'It wasn't like that before you came. It was different – it was better. Don't think you're going to be our friend 'cause you're not. Clear off, go on. Find somebody else to hang around with.'

The gang ran off, kicking stones and shouting. Ivor dragged slowly after them, looking miserably down into the gutter. How could it be his fault?

Geoffrey Simpson

Hymn
'Shalom' (*Come and Praise* Vol 2, 141)

Prayer
Dear God,
Help us to avoid bullying in all its forms. Give us the strength to act justly and fairly in our own lives. Give us the courage to show kindness and consideration to those who are being unfairly treated.
Amen

The Bible says
Thou shalt not kill, thou shalt not steal, thou shalt not covet, and any other commandment there may be, are all summed up in one rule, 'Love your neighbour as yourself.' Love cannot wrong a neighbour; therefore the whole law is summed up in love.

Romans 13: 9–10

Class presentation ideas

Preparation
Prepare a reading (or drama) based on the story of Jesus and Zacchaeus the tax collector (Luke 19: 1–10).

Presentation
Set the scene and explain some of the background to wartime evacuations. This could be followed by a reading of the core material. When the audience has had a chance to absorb this, the presenters could begin a 'question and answer' dialogue, as follows:

Presenter 1   What do you think Ivor wanted more than anything else?
Presenter 2   Was it fair to blame him for the problems?
Presenter 3   Why did the gang do so?
Presenter 4   What should John, Jim and Brian have done? What would *you* have done?
Presenter 5   What might have happened if the boys had been friendly to Ivor?

Conclusion
The final question could be developed in a number of ways, depending on the circumstances – for example, if there is a new pupil in the class or the school, or if there are recent arrivals in the local community.

1   Discuss the feelings and fears of all 'newcomers' – and how we can help strangers to feel welcome and at home.
2   Think about the benefits for both newcomers and the established community which come from sharing ideas, culture, traditions etc.
3   Stress the importance of not judging others or seeing them as 'outsiders', but rather seeing them as people like ourselves – this leads naturally into the story of Jesus and Zacchaeus, where Jesus saw Zacchaeus as a person, not just a hated tax-collector.

32 This is the key

Presenter's note
Today's poem needs a lot of thinking about. Perhaps its most important message is that we should never forget how important the 'little things' in life are.

Introduction
Sometimes in our big, busy, bustling world it is easy to forget how important little things are. This morning's poem is a reminder.

Core material

> This is the key of the Kingdom:
> In that Kingdom there is a city.
> In that city there is a town.
> In that town there is a street.
> In that street there is a lane.
> In that lane there is a yard.
> In that yard there is a house.
> In that house there is a room.
> In that room there is a bed.
> On that bed there is a basket.
> In that basket there are some flowers.
> Flowers in a basket.
> Basket on a bed.
> Bed in the room.
> Room in the house.
> House in the yard.
> Yard in the lane.
> Lane in the street.
> Street in the town.
> Town in the city.
> City in the Kingdom.
> Of the Kingdom this is the key.

Anon

Hymn
'Think of a world without any flowers' (*Come and Praise* Vol 1, 17)

Prayer
Dear God,
Give us the wisdom to judge things for their worth. Let us value the beauty of

nature, the joy of the seasons, the treasure of friends. Let us value the important little things in our lives.   Amen

The Bible says
Think of ships; large they may be, yet even when driven by strong gales they can be directed by a tiny rudder on whatever course the helmsman chooses.

James 3: 4–5

Class presentation ideas

Preparation
Some children could be asked to make a collection of 'little things.' According to season and availability these could be very wide-ranging: seeds, flowers, acorns, a wedding ring, mouthpiece of a wind instrument, a book, pen, a small gift which is precious not because of its monetary value but because of why it was given and who it was given by.

Development
Presenters comment on the significance of the objects on display. This part of the assembly will depend very largely on what has been collected.

Conclusion
Draw out the moral that if the small things are not right, then neither will the larger ones be.

33 Out in the fields with God

Presenter's note
Some unmanned railway crossings in the USA used to bear the simple slogan
of STOP! LOOK! LISTEN! This seems like good advice for assemblies too.

Introduction
Look around you. Now listen very carefully. Think about what sights please
you. Think about what sounds please you. Listen to the following poem and
try and see, in your mind's eye, exactly what the poet is describing.

Core material
> The little cares that fret'd me,
> I lost them yesterday,
> Among the fields above the sea,
> Among the winds at play,
> Among the lowing of the herds,
> The rustling of the trees,
> Among the singing of the birds,
> The humming of the bees.
>
> The foolish fears of what might pass,
> I cast them all away,
> Among the clover-scented grass,
> Among the new-mown hay,
> Among the hushing of the corn,
> Where drowsy poppies nod,
> Where ill thoughts die and good are born –
> Out in the fields with God.

Anon

Hymn
'Morning has broken' (*Come and Praise* Vol 1, 1)

Prayer
Dear God,
Open our eyes to see the beautiful things around us; let our ears hear your gifts
of sounds. Free our minds from worries over things about which we can do
nothing. Help us to be thankful for each day, treating it as your special gift.
   Amen

The Bible says
Live like men who are at home in daylight, for where light is, there all goodness springs up, all justice and truth.

Ephesians, 5: 9

Class presentation ideas
This could be one of those assemblies which might be described as 'sensory' and 'sensitive'.

We rarely make full use of our senses to appreciate things around us. One reason, of course, is that when things become familiar we simply stop 'seeing' or 'hearing' them.

This poem could open an assembly which seeks to re-focus our attention on things of value. The presenters might begin with a choral delivery of the poem, then concentrate on visual and aural appreciation.

Included in this could be more poems: 'things I enjoy seeing and hearing'; paintings; pictures; photographs; interesting and beautiful objects; pieces of music – either played on record or tape, or performed by presenters on recorders and percussion; tapes of bird songs, a friend or relative's voice.

Such an assembly should not only give a great deal of pleasure, it would also be useful in starting off chains of thought in other classes so that the theme can be pursued in other areas of the school.

34 Whose dog?

Presenter's note
This morning's poem is based upon an incident when Robert Louis Stevenson saw a man ill-treating a dog at Pitlochry.

Introduction
It is a sad fact that there are many bullies in the world. This morning we are going to hear a poem in which a man had the perfect answer to a bully.

Core material

> In Scotland, grey and craggy,
> Down by old Pitlochry,
> A man was walking,
> A day long ago.
> There cross'd his path
> Another
> Who, with hand and foot,
> Beat and kicked
> A thin and aged dog.
> "Stop that!"
> Cried our hero
> Without a second's thought.
> "What?"
> Snarled the bully.
> "Who are you to tell me
> What to do? It's
> Not your dog."
> "No,"
> Replied our friend.
> "The dog belongs to God
> And I am here to protect it."

Joe Spink

Hymn
'Give us hope Lord' (*Come and Praise* Vol 2, 87)

Prayer
Dear God,
Teach us to control our minds and bodies. Help us to keep our tempers. Give us the wisdom to see that all bullying is cruel. Please guide us at all times.
  Amen

The Bible says
It is the fault of a violent man that quarrels start.
                              Proverbs 29 v 2

Class presentation ideas
Spell out the word BULLY on large placards or sheets of paper.

Presenters read or act out various examples of bullying, eg playground situations, occasions when the strong 'pick on' the weak etc. Older children might think of situations where powerful countries 'bully' smaller neighbours.

The poem could be used to conclude the assembly. Bullying is a hard problem to solve, but the poem does at least prompt thought on the issue.

35 The house

Presenter's note
This story is about *values*.

Introduction
Everybody makes mistakes but some people learn from them. This morning's story is about a lady who had a dream which taught her a lot!

Core material
Mrs Ponsonby lived in a splendid house. It had 20 bedrooms and 10 rooms downstairs. There was a swimming pool outside in the enormous garden. The garden itself consisted of an orchard, several green-houses, a huge lawn and dozens of beautifully-kept flower beds. The man who kept the garden in such magnificent condition was Henry. He had been Mrs Ponsonby's gardener for many years.

Mrs Ponsonby considered herself to be a very important person in the district. She was invited to all the best parties, never went to the theatre unless it was in the best seats, and seldom went anywhere unless it was in her husband's pale grey Rolls Royce.

She rarely spoke to Henry or any other of the servants. When she did it was usually just to give them a sharp command. Whether they were happy or contented never crossed her mind. She paid them all the lowest possible wages.

'Oh she's not so bad really,' Henry used to say when the others moaned about Mrs Ponsonby. 'She lets me get on in the garden in peace doesn't she?'

'You're too soft Henry, that's your trouble,' replied George the butler. 'I bet she has no idea that you do poor old Mrs Crampitt's garden for nothing in your spare time. And what about the way you keep the churchyard looking so good – not to mention the vicar's garden.'

'Oh, anybody would do that,' said Henry shyly.

'I bet anybody wouldn't help half the village with advice about their gardens – and hard work if necessary. And all for nothing. I bet old ma Ponsonby has never done anything for nothing in her whole life.'

'Oh she's not so bad,' smiled Henry again.

It was about a week later that Mrs Ponsonby had the dream.

She dreamt that she had died. A short while later she was met by St Peter at the gates to Heaven.

'Welcome,' said St Peter. 'If you'd like to come with me I'll show you to your new house.'

Remembering the house she had left on earth Mrs Ponsonby smiled and stepped into the waiting car.

Soon it was travelling down a wide road with pleasant houses on either side. After a time the road began to drop to where the houses were very much poorer. Finally the car pulled up in front of a very mean looking house. It was unpainted and scruffly; it looked cold and damp.

'This is it,' said St Peter.

'But . . .' spluttered Mrs Ponsonby, 'but . . .'

'Surprised, are you?' went on St Peter. 'Well, you see, the material you give us to work with from your time on earth decides what sort of a house you have up here. Kindness, consideration for others, thoughtfulness, unselfishness – all these things help to build your house up here. I'm afraid you didn't give us very much to build with.'

Just at that moment the sun broke through the clouds and shone down on a magnificient house which stood on top of a nearby hill.

St Peter saw Mrs Ponsonby looking at it enviously.

'Ah – that belongs to a friend of yours. He died today too, so he'll be moving in shortly. He gave us an awful lot to build with when he was down there.'

'But . . . you said it belonged to a friend of mine . . .'

'Yes, yes – Henry, your old gardener.'

Mrs Ponsonby woke up with a start. As soon as she did so she began to think
. . .

Hymn
'Simple Gifts' (*Come and Praise* Vol 2, 97)

Prayer

Dear God,
We can all look back and see the mistakes we have made.
Please
Give us the wisdom to avoid making them again.
Help us to be attentive, caring and kind.

Amen

The Bible says
'*Whoever wants to be first must be the willing slave of all. For even the Son of Man did not come to be served but to serve, and to give up His life as a ransom for many.*'

Mark 10: 44–45

Class presentation ideas
Two or three child presenters could read the story as their colleagues mime the action.

Apart from the main theme there is plenty of scope to expand for dramatic purposes – Mrs P at a party; the servants' chat; in the churchyard; the villagers' gardens etc.

36 Following the fashion

Presenter's note
This is an old fold tale which carries on the moral and tradition of stories like 'The Emperor's New Clothes'.

Introduction
Sometimes we need to ask for advice, but we should always be careful about accepting it from someone we don't know, as this story shows.

Core material
Alfredo stood in front of the mirror. First he turned to one side, then the other.

'I look really smart,' he said to himself, smoothing down the sides of his long coat and adjusting his wide-brimmed hat. 'How important it is to be dressed in the height of fashion. Now, when I go to town everybody will be impressed with how I look.'

Satisfied that he could not look smarter, nor more in fashion, Alfredo set off to town. It was a very long journey and he had not gone far when he came across a man sitting on a bench beside a river. Feeling in need of a rest, Alfredo sat down next to the man.

'Good morning,' he said.

'Good morning,' replied the stranger.

The two men began to talk about this and that and soon Alfredo, who was very vain, told the stranger that he was going into town.

'I like to go there from time to time,' he said, 'and I always make sure that I wear the smartest and most fashionable clothes.'

'No good going like that then,' replied the stranger rather rudely.

'What do you mean?'

'Well I was in town the day before yesterday. Fashions have changed enormously. You'd really look out of place in those clothes.'

'Really? But what is in fashion . . . please . . . tell me at once!'

'Well,' said the stranger, 'first of all there is this strange idea that everybody wears their hat back-to-front. Secondly people are wearing coats without sleeves and, believe it or not, nobody is wearing shoes this year.'

Alfredo could hardly believe his ears. Still, if this man had just come from the town he must know what he was talking about. Fancy if he'd gone there dressed like this! What a misfit everybody would have thought him.

'Thank you,' he said to the stranger. 'Thank you very much for your advice.'

When the stranger had gone, Alfredo continued on his way. Before reaching the town he altered the shape of his hat so that he could wear it back to front, he tore the sleeves out of his coat and he threw his shoes away.

When he got to town everybody stared at him, and then roared with laughter.

'How ridiculous,' they shouted. 'Why on earth are you dressed like that?'

Hymn

'From the tiny ant' (*Come and Praise* Vol 2, 79)

Prayer

Let us have the good sense to recognise foolish actions.
Let us have the ability to think for ourselves.
Let us be grateful for the talents and common sense we are given.
Amen

The Bible says

Be most careful how you conduct yourselves;
like sensible men, not like simpletons.

Ephesians 5: 15

Class presentation ideas

Children of all junior school ages will enjoy acting this story. It could be linked with 'The Emperor's New Clothes' (this could not be acted for obvious reasons (!) but it might be narrated here).

Another choice of story could be the Bible story of the foolish bridesmaids at the wedding (Matthew, 25: 10–12). In this instance unpreparedness links with foolishness.

37 The artist

Presenter's note
This is a story of a man with gifts using them for the benefit of others – and a greedy man getting his just deserts.

Introduction
This morning's story is about an artist who could paint magic pictures, and a selfish nobleman who thought that this might help him to get even richer. However, things didn't quite work out as the nobleman expected – as we shall see.

Core material
Chew Moy Lam was an artist – but no ordinary artist. He had magic powers so when he painted a picture he could turn it into reality, and then give it away to the person of his choice. Now, because he was a generous man he was always painting bowls of rice, loaves of bread, plates of fish – and then giving these away to all the poor people he knew.

Not surprisingly people admired and respected Chew Moy Lam and hardly anybody ever asked him to 'paint a meal' for them. They knew he worked as hard as he could and shared his magic powers for the benefit of all.

However there is usually one person who upsets things – and this time this person's name was Tien Chi. Tien Chi was a powerful nobleman. Stories of what Chew Moy Lam could do soon reached his large and extravagantly-furnished palace.

'Bring this man to me,' Tien Chi commanded his guards. They set off to do their master's bidding. Chew Moy Lam was not hard to find and he made no effort to resist the soldiers. Soon he was standing in front of the smirking Tien Chi.

'I've heard about you,' said the nobleman, 'and I've got something for you to do.'

At this point he snapped his fingers and had a large piece of paper and some paints brought to him. Handing these to Chew Moy Lam he said, 'Get started – paint a thousand crowns – and then give them to me.'

'And what if I won't?' asked Chew Moy Lam.

'You'll go straight to prison and you'll stay there until you see sense,' replied Tien Chi.

'Very well, you'd better send me to prison,' said the artist.

Within minutes the artist was bundled into a damp, dark prison cell. The paper and paints were thrown in after him. With a loud clang a soldier slammed the cell door and locked it.

Chew Moy Lam waited until the guard had tramped away, and then he set to work. First of all he tore the paper in half. Then he began to paint. He worked quickly and when he had finished his picture he smiled with satisfaction. Then taking the other half of the paper, he painted a second picture.

Chew Moy Lam laid this second picture on the floor by his feet. It was a painting of a key. Closing his eyes, he paused, and then looked down. There on the floor was a real key. He picked it up and unlocked the cell door. Then, with the first painting in his hand, he marched out into the corridor.

'Hey . . . what . . .?' gasped an astonished guard.

'Take me to your master, at once,' said Chew Moy Lam. He waved the paper at the guard. 'I have something to give him.'

The guard hurried ahead and within a few minutes the artist stood once again in front of the disdainful nobleman.

'So – it didn't take you long to come to your sense,' said Tien Chi. 'Very wise. Come on then, hand over the picture!'

Silently Chew Moy Lam gave his painting to Tien Chi. The nobleman's mouth dropped as he looked at it. He just had time to see that he was looking at a puff of smoke – before he disappeared into it!

No sooner had Tien Chi vanished than the guards and courtiers crowded round Chew Moy Lam and slapped his back in thanks and congratulations. They had all been desperately afraid of their cruel master – and now the magic artist had freed them!

Hymn
'I'm going to paint' (*Come and Praise* Vol 2, 83)

Prayer
Lord, help us to learn from this morning's story, the value of using our gifts for good. Thank you for the gifts and abilities we possess. We ask your guidance in helping us to appreciate the gifts of others.

Amen

The Bible says
Pass no judgement and you will not be judged; do not condemn and you will not be condemned; acquit and you will be acquitted; give and gifts will be given to you . . . for whatever measures you deal out to others will be dealt to you in return.

Luke 6: 37–38

Class presentation ideas
This is a lovely story to dramatise. Paintings of a bowl of rice, a loaf of bread, a key and a puff of smoke should be done in advance. The real things should then be acquired – some rice, bread, a key and some talcum powder or other suitable material for a 'puff of smoke' – and introduced at appropriate times in the story.

38 Jumping to conclusions

Presenter's note
This assembly's salutary tale will undoubtedly strike some chords. How often do we see faults in others when we want to – and how often are we mistaken.

Introduction
Have you ever lost something and thought: 'somebody's taken it'. I'm sure you have, like one of the people in this morning's story.

Core material
Jacob and Hans lived next door to each other. Both were woodcutters. They spent long hours chopping down trees in the wood. Each had a prized axe, sharpened to a fine edge with a blade as sharp as any knife.

One morning Jacob got up as usual. After breakfast he prepared to go to work. He went last of all to the space on the porch where he kept his axe. It wasn't there!

'I always leave it here,' said Jacob to himself. 'It is never anywhere else. I always leave it in the same . . . somebody's stolen it! But who would do such a thing? It could only be one person!'

At that moment Hans came out of his own door, carrying his own axe. He muttered 'Morning' but didn't look at Jacob as he hurried off into the woods.

'He's bound to deny it if I ask him . . . or accuse him,' thought Jacob. 'I'll just watch and see how he behaves.'

That night when Hans came back Jacob was leaning on the porch.

'Had a hard day Hans?' he asked.

'Hmm,' Hans mumbled, and hurried into the house.

'Ha – he's afraid to talk to me – guilty conscience,' thought Jacob.

Jacob used his spare axe for the next few days and watched Hans closely. Hans seemed guilty in every way – how he moved, how he looked, how he spoke – or didn't speak.

Then one night Jacob went to cut some logs for his fire.

'That Hans,' he thought to himself. 'Any day now he'll come and confess his guilt.'

Pushing through the grass Jacob came to his log pile. He was just preparing to cut into a piece of wood when there, lying on the ground . . . he saw his prized, favourite axe.

'Oh no! Now I remember . . . it was last . . .'

Next morning Jacob was on his porch when Hans came out.

'Morning Hans,' said Jacob.

'Morning,' muttered Hans, but he didn't look at Jacob as he hurried off into the woods. Somehow – the way he said it, the way he moved, the way he looked. He didn't seem guilty at all!

Hymn
'Make us worthy Lord' (*Come and Praise* Vol 2, 94)

Prayer
Lord, so often we behave badly for so many reasons. Please help us to think before we act hastily and pass judgement on others.
    Amen

The Bible says
A fool rushes into a house, while a man of experience hangs back politely.
Ecclesiasticus 22:22

Class presentation ideas
The theme of this assembly will be very familiar to children of this age. 'He did it . . . she did it' etc are phrases well-known to all teachers.

    The story might therefore be used as a centre piece of an assembly on good manners in the community, in this instance in the school. This should emphasise also the qualities of mutual trust and honest speech.

39 Happy Families

Presenter's note
Saying cruel things can cause a great deal of distress, and have far-reaching consequences – sometimes for the person who spoke thoughtlessly in the first place.

Introduction
In some ways this morning's story is quite cruel – but then so often many things which we say to other people are cruel too. Perhaps this story will help us to think before we speak in such situations.

Core material
Have you ever played the card game 'Happy Families'? If so, you will know that it involves collecting groups of cards which all belong to one family. The player who gets the most 'families' by the end of the game is the winner.

People of all ages can play the game and it is good fun. Sometimes, however, the real happiness of families can be spoilt by thoughtlessness and an unkind remark.

The Roberts family lived in a nice comfortable house. There was Mr Roberts and his wife, the twins Shane and Vicki, and little Darren. Oh, and of course there was also Grandad.

Grandad was Mr Roberts' father and he had recently come to live with the family after the death of his wife. He was quite a frail old man with wispy white hair and he couldn't always do things as well as he had been able to when he was younger.

'Your father does annoy me,' said Mrs Roberts to her husband one day. 'He really does.'

Mr Roberts, who was reading the paper, put it down and looked up.

'Oh, how's that my dear? How's that?'

'Well you know how I like everybody to be on time for meals – I have to call him and call him before he comes.'

'Hmm – but he is getting a bit deaf you know.'

'And there's another thing,' went on Mrs Roberts, ignoring her husband. 'Its the way he eats. He drops things on the cloth and he doesn't always hold his knife properly. In fact he eats so badly I sometimes think we ought to get him a trough!'

Mr Roberts looked sadly at his wife, but didn't say anything. Neither of them noticed that Shane had been passing the room where they were – and had heard everything.

Later that night Mrs Roberts heard an awful lot of banging and hammering coming from Shane's room. When she went to see what was happening she found him surrounded by pieces of wood, a saw, some nails and a hammer.

'Shane! What on earth are you doing?' she gasped.

'Oh it's all right Mum,' he said. 'I'm just making a trough for when you get old.'

Hymn
'Black and White' (*Come and Praise* Vol 1, 67)

Prayer

> Let us pray that we have a healthy mind which sees goodness
> where it can.
> Let such a mind not avoid unpleasant things but seek to put them right.
> Let such a mind not be too concerned with that person 'I'.

The Bible says
The tongue – it is a small member but it can make huge claims. What an immense stack of timber can be set ablaze by the tiniest spark! And the tongue is in effect a fire.

James 3: 5–6

Class presentation ideas

Preparation
Label a large exercise book 'Tongue stories'. This will contain readings for the assembly – the 'Happy families' core material and other suitable tales. A number of Aesop's fables are appropriate here, eg 'Cry Wolf', 'The Donkey in the Lion's Skin', 'The Hunter and the Woodsman', 'The Fox without a Tail'.

Development
Presenters read one or more stories from the book as the rest of the group act them out.

Conclusion
Following this part of the assembly, the presenter could move on to consider the positive and valuable aspects of the tongue – how it can be used to pass on information, to give encouragement, to express sympathy and love, to entertain.

40 Doing a job properly

Presenter's note
Richard III lost his life when his horse fell in battle . . . because it had not been shoed properly. There is plenty of scope for variation on this theme and the story which follows offers one example. Extension possibilities are equally good, based on St Luke's comment that: 'A man who can be trusted with a small job can be trusted with a big one'.

Introduction
Do we always do a job as well as we are able to? If we don't, what sort of thing happens? This story tells us one such case.

Core material
It was the night of the Barn Dance. Jimmy and Steve were both going, and as the afternoon crept away they were keen to finish work so that they could go home and wash and change.

The two young men were both carpenters. They were putting up cupboards in new houses on a new estate.

'I'm never going to get these cupboards put up properly by 5 o'clock,' thought Jimmy, as he looked at the wood piled round him. 'First I've got to drill the holes, then put the wall plugs in, then screw everything up. It'll take . . .'

Jimmy had an idea. What if he drilled the holes, put the wall plugs in the holes – and then hit the screws in with a hammer? It would be much quicker, nobody would ever know, and he'd get home with plenty of time to get ready for the Barn Dance.

'Right,' he muttered to himself, 'now for it.'

Meanwhile Steve was at work in a second house, but he thought rather differently.

'If I'm going to do the job properly I'll never get finished by 5 o'clock. Still its better to make sure these cupboards are firmly fixed to the wall or there might be an accident some time.'

Laying out his drill, wall plugs, screws and screw driver, Steve began to fix the first cupboard. Shortly after 5 o'clock he heard a shout. Looking out of the window he saw Jimmy striding by.

'Not finished, slowcoach?' shouted Jimmy, 'You'll be late for the dance.'

'But . . . ?' began Steve. He knew Jimmy had the same amount of work to do as he had. He just couldn't have finished, unless he had cheated.

Later that night the streamers blew in the breeze caused by the swirling of the dancers in the big village hall. Fiddlers played their foot-tapping tunes.

When Steve arrived at the hall the first person he saw was Jimmy – obviously having a great time.

'Pity it took you so long to get here,' shouted Jimmy.

'Maybe,' replied Steve,' but there's somebody here wants to see you.

A few seconds later Jimmy was facing a very angry foreman.

'The people who are buying that house you are working on went to look at it this evening. When they tried the cupboards in the kitchen to see how firm they were – they fell off the wall. I'm afraid we can do without your sort of workman – you're fired!'

Hymn
'The Building Song' (*Come and Praise* Vol 1, 61)

Prayer
Dear God, Help us when we are given a job to do. Give us the patience, determination and skill to do it to the best of our ability. Help us to resist temptation when there seems to be a 'short cut' instead of doing the job properly.

The Bible says
He is like a man who had the sense to build his house on rock. The rain came down, the floods rose, the wind blew, and beat upon that house; but it did not fall, because its foundations were on rock. But what of the man who hears these words of mine and does not act upon them? He is like a man who was foolish enough to build his house on sand. The rain came down, the floods rose, the wind blew, and beat upon that house; down it fell with a great crash.

Matthew 7: 24–27

Class presentation ideas
The core material here could be used as just one example of what is likely to happen if people do not do their jobs as well as they should.

The story of Richard III could also be recited or acted out by the group:

> For want of a nail a shoe was lost
> For want of a shoe a horse was lost
> For want of a horse a rider was lost
> For want of a rider a battle was lost
> For want of a battle a kingdom was lost
> And all for the want of a horseshoe nail.

Benjamin Franklin

41 The brothers

Presenter's note
This folk tale is about three brothers who used their initiative to care for their ageing parents.

Introduction
This story is about three brothers and how they were able to show their appreciation for all the loving care their parents had given them.

Core material
The three brothers sat at the table and looked at each other.

'Our father and mother are getting old and should not work so hard,' said Ben.

'That's true – and this land is so poor and worked out,' replied Simon.

'How can we help, we know nothing but toiling on the land ourselves?' muttered Peter.

'I suggest we leave home, make our fortunes, and return to look after our father and mother for the rest of their days,' said Ben at last.

The boys' parents were very sad when they heard that their children were leaving home. However they had to work so hard on their land to scratch a living that there wasn't much time to talk about it.

Soon the sons stood at the crossroads in the centre of the village.

'We'll each go our different ways, and we'll meet here again in a year and a day,' said Simon.

Shaking hands, each of them went his different way.

A year passed quickly. Sure enough each brother was on time for the meeting.

'I'm not rich,' said Ben, 'but I've spent the year as a sailor. My captain was so pleased with my work that he gave me a telescope which can see anything.'

'Fancy you being a sailor,' laughed Simon. 'I'm not rich either but I know how to build good ships after a year working in the docks.'

'I can't say I'm rich either,' said Peter. 'I've been working for a locksmith. I can make, or get into, any lock, but I haven't much money.'

The parents were delighted to see the boys back. They didn't mind about the money, but the farm was even poorer now, and they were even more tired. However they told their sons of some news which had shocked the village.

'A visiting army plundered the village, and kidnapped the king's daughter. The king has promised that any man who can find his daughter and bring her back, may marry her.'

The next day the brothers went to see the king and heard the whole sad story.

'I think we may be able to help you, your Majesty,' said Ben.

Putting his telescope to his eye he saw that the princess was imprisoned in a castle on an island.

'I can build a ship which will get us there,' said Simon.

'And there isn't a lock that I can't unpick,' said Peter proudly.

Within a few weeks the ship was made and the brothers set out. They slipped their boat quietly on to the beach of the island when it was dark. Then they made their way to the castle. The king who owned it was so sure that nobody could get through the huge locks that hung on its main door, that he didn't bother with many guards.

Dodging the sleepy soldiers on guard Peter skilfully picked the great locks. Soon the brothers found the princess. They woke her gently and crept back with her to their boat.

The king was absolutely delighted when his daughter returned. Then his face clouded with worry.

'But . . . there are three of you. My daughter can't marry three men!'

'Your Majesty,' said Ben. 'Your daughter might not even want to marry any of us. Perhaps you could help us in another way.'

'Please tell me how,' said the king.

Minutes later the brothers were the owners of a large and fertile stretch of land. Within days they moved their parents from the ramshackle old farm, and built them a new house on their land. They worked very hard to farm it and make it prosperous, whilst their proud parents enjoyed a well-earned rest.

Hymn
'From the tiny ant' (*Come and Praise* Vol 2, 79)

Prayer
Dear God, Thank you for our mothers and father, and all the love, care and time they give to us. Help us to be grateful, and show our appreciation by the way we behave.

Amen

The Bible says
'*Honour your father and mother.*'

Exodus 20: 16

Class presentation ideas
Begin with the presenters talking about their parents: 'I like it when my dad . . .' 'I like to help my mum/dad with . . .' 'One of the best times I have with my mum/dad is when . . .' and so on.

Having focused attention on 'mums and dads' the core material might then be narrated or acted. The assembly might then switch back to the children's own experience with the presenters again detailing ways in which they help their own parents.

42 To give is to receive

Presenter's note
This story is based on an old Japanese folk tale in which generosity and its rewards are the theme. Running parallel with this is the idea that great things can grow from very small beginnings.

Introduction
This morning's story is an old Japanese folk tale. It tells how one good turn deserves another, and another, and another . . .

Core material
Shobei had done a hard day's work on the farm when he fell over on his way home. As he was getting up he noticed that a piece of straw had caught between his fingers. Perched on the end of the straw was a dragonfly. No matter how Shobei wiggled the straw the dragonfly wouldn't move.

'Look, mummy, look, look,' a child's voice suddenly startled Shobei. Glancing upwards he saw a small boy tugging his mother's arm and pointing at the dragonfly on the straw.

'Could I . . .' began the boy.

'I know what you're going to say,' interrupted Shobei. 'Of course you can have it.'

So saying he handed the straw and the dragonfly over to the little boy.

'That's so kind of you,' said the child's mother. 'Please take these in exchange.'

She handed Shobei three of the ripe, juicy oranges she was carrying. Shobei thanked her and continued on his way home. He hadn't gone very far before he came across a merchant, staggering along in the heat and weighed down by a pile of different cloths.

'You look to me as if you could do with a drink,' said Shobei. 'Try one of these oranges.'

The merchant accepted an orange and ate it thankfully. He was even more pleased when Shobei gave him a second orange to make sure his thirst was quenched.

'That's very generous of you,' he said to Shobei. 'The least I can do is give you something in exchange. Here, have one of my best pieces of cloth.'

Soon Shobei was on his way again, the beautifully-coloured cloth thrown over one arm. After a while he had to move to the side of the road as a fine carriage swept by. No sooner had it done so than, with much shouting and clouds of dust, it was brought to a halt. Two of the guards leapt from the back of the carriage and hurried towards Shobei.

'Come with us,' one of them ordered.

Seconds later Shobei was staring into the back of the carriage. He gasped when he saw who was sitting there. It was the Emperor's daughter, the beautiful Princess Lotus Flower. Shobei bowed low.

The princess spoke in a soft and lilting voice.

'I couldn't help noticing that lovely cloth you were carrying as we past you. Would you let me buy it from you please?'

'Certainly not, you Majesty,' replied Shobei. 'Nothing would give me greater pleasure than to give you the cloth.'

So saying the bowed again and handed the cloth to the princess.

'You are a most kind man,' said the princess. 'Please accept a gift in return.'

At a signal from the princess one of the guards handed Shobei a small bag. Then the carriage went on its way.

Carefully Shobei opened the bag and looked inside. He had never seen anything like it. The bag was full of gold! He hurried home to tell everyone the good news.

Shortly after this Shobei used his money to buy some fields. Then he gathered all the people of his village together and told them that he was going to share out the fields between them. This he did and not only did Shobei become a very wealthy man, but everybody in his village did too; and to think it all started with a piece of straw . . .

Hymn
'The best gift' (*Come and Praise* Vol 1, 59)

Prayer
Dear God, Help us to say thank-you today for oportunities. Opportunities to make friends, to give a little happiness by being as kind and generous as we can, to learn more about ourselves and others.

Thank you for the opportunity to come together today in this, our school. Help us to make the most of all that is offered to us here.

Amen

The Bible says
Pass no judgement, and you will not be judged; do not condemn and you will not be condemned; acquit and you will be acquitted; give and gifts will be given to you . . . for whatever measure you deal out to others will be dealt to you in return.

Luke 6: 37–38

Class presentation ideas
This is one of those episodic stories which could be adapted for dramatisation very easily, and which could be presented by any junior school age group.

For heightened effect a display of some Japanese artifacts or pictures would be useful, as would a map showing where Japan is.

43 Fig tale

Presenter's note
The stories of Nasr-ud-Din Hodja are very famous in Turkey. Here is a tale of his quick-wittedness.

Introduction
We all enjoy a funny story. We also admire people who, when caught in a tricky position, keep their sense of humour and can laugh at themselves. Today's story is about Nasr-ud-Din, one of Turkey's most famous 'characters'.

Core material
The great conqueror Timur Leng often sought the company of Nasr-ud-Din.

'You make me laugh,' he used to say. 'You, with your ridiculous schemes and even more ridiculous adventures.'

Now, although Timur Leng liked Nasr-ud-Din, he was still a proud and fierce warrior lord who had to be respected and treated carefully. One day Nasr-ud-Din was going to see Timur, so he decided to take a bunch of very ripe beetroot with him as a present. On his way, however, he passed a stall where a trader was selling figs.

'I think that would be a better present,' thought Nasr-ud-Din. Minutes later he had sold his beetroot and was on his way with a bunch of figs. Half an hour later he stood in front of a furious Timur.

'How dare you?' shouted the great warrior. 'From all over the world people bring me gifts of gold and silver – and you dare to offer me rubbish like that!'

'But . . .'

'Silence! You there – guards – throw these figs back in this scoundrel's face.'

Trying to hide their smiles the soldiers picked up the figs and began pelting Nasr-ud-Din with them.

'Thank you – oh, thank you,' he called out.

At once Timur ordered the fig-throwing to stop.

'Thank you?' he said, 'why are you saying thank you when you are being pelted – are you mad?'

'Thank you . . . thank you . . .' went on Nasr-ud-Din. 'No your majesty, I'm not mad. I'm just saying thank you for the fact that I did not bring the ripe beetroot!'

Hymn
'You shall go out with joy' (*Come and Praise* Vol 2, 98)

Prayer

'Give me a sense of humour Lord,
Give me the grace to see a joke,
To get some happiness from life
And pass it on to other folk.'
(from an anonymous prayer found in Chester Cathedral)

The Bible says

Rich and poor, they are lighthearted, and always have a smile on their faces.
Ecclesiasticus 26: 4

Class presentation ideas

The emphasis of this assembly is on wit and humour. When the audience is in place in the hall the presenters might open proceedings by telling some jokes. (The teacher should check this material first.)

This provides a natural introduction to a dramatisation of the Hodja story.

When the play is over one or two of the presenters might make comments for future thought. These might include:

- How important it is for us to be able to laugh at ourselves, not take ourselves too seriously.
- How important it is to laugh *with* people, and not at them.
- A cheerful companion is always enjoyed more than a miserable one. We should try to present this side of ourselves to the world despite the difficulties and disappointments we all suffer.

Follow up

A very useful bookshop is Soma Books, 38 Kennington Lane, London SE11 4LS. It stocks a good selection of books of folk tales.

44 Not such a joke

Presenter's note
We should laugh *with* people, and not *at* them, as this story shows.

Introduction
I expect you have all heard somebody poking fun at somebody else in the playground. Cruel things are often said when this happens.

Today's story is about a king who made fun of an ugly old woman – until he learned his lesson!

Core material
The king was in the habit of sitting near a window in his palace. One day a very ugly old woman passed by.

'Ha,' cried the king, 'I've never seen anybody so ugly.'

He pointed to the old woman, and all his courtiers felt that they had better laugh too.

Every week the old woman went by at the same time, and every week the king laughed and made fun of her.

Now, unknown to the king, the old woman had magical powers. She could change herself into any shape.

'That king needs to be taught a lesson,' she thought to herself. 'He's thoughtless, cruel and full of his own importance.'

So saying, the old woman changed herself into a beautiful girl. Then she went to the palace and asked if she could work as a maid for the queen. Everybody was so impressed with her looks and cheerful smile that she got the job straight away.

A few days later, as the girl passed a plate, she touched the queen's hand. At once the queen's nose began to grow. It grew and grew until it was absolutely enormous. The queen screamed for help – and the beautiful maid vanished.

The king was desperate. The queen wouldn't let herself be seen anywhere and nobody could help him – or her. He sat at his window and looked out miserably. Sure enough, the ugly old woman eventually came along.

This time the king was in no mood to laugh any anybody, but when she looked up at him and he saw the expression in her eyes he thought, Could it be? Could she?

'The king has asked if you would kindly come and see him,' said the two courtiers who had been sent after the old woman.

'Yes,' she replied.

A little while later the king and the old woman faced each other in the palace.

'You did it, didn't you?' said the king. 'I just know you did it.'

'Yes, I did it,' said the old woman, 'to teach you a lesson.'

'Will you, please . . . How can I . . . please' muttered the king.

'I feel sorry for your wife,' went on the old woman, 'and of course I'll restore her beauty – if you've learned your lesson.'

'I have,' pleaded the king. 'Believe me, I have.'

'Remember then,' said the old woman – and vanished instantly.

At once there was a cry of delight from the queen's bedroom. Her nose was back to normal!

After that the king never, ever made fun or laughed at other people's faults.

Hymn
'Break Out' (*Come and Praise* Vol 2, 91)

Prayer
Forgive me, O God, for those times when I have thoughtlessly and unkindly made fun of others. Teach me to consider the feelings of other people and to keep silent if I cannot use my words and actions for good.

Amen

The Bible says
The wisdom from above is in the first place pure; and then peace loving, considerate and open to reason; it is straightforward and sincere; rich in mercy and in the kindly deeds that are its fruit.

James 3: 17–18

Class presentation ideas

Preparation
Prepare some large cards which spell out:

BE KIND NOT CRUEL

The presenters could then produce this story with a combination of narrative and mime. As the first part unfolds, one child at a time could reveal the letters CRUEL slowly and in order.

Conclusion
When the denouement has been reached the other card holders could turn their letter cards round so that the clear simple message is revealed to all.

This story is adapted from one which appears in *Armenian Folk Tales and Fables*, by Charles Downing, published by Oxford University Press. This book is an excellent source for stories, fables, and 'sayings'.

45 The game

Presenter's note
This is one of those clever tales 'with a twist', in which the deserving are rewarded.

Introduction
Today's story is about a card game and what happened when a new player came to the table.

Core material
'That's my trick.'
'Well played.'
'Our turn to win tonight.'
'That's a lot of money you owe us.'
'If only you hadn't had such good clubs.'

Every night a conversation like this took place at the club in which rich merchants played cards. Every night large sums of money were gambled for and changed hands.

Meanwhile, just along the steet from the club, lived a desperately poor mother of six children. Although he worked as many hours as he possibly could, her husband could never quite make enough money to make ends meet. The poor woman often thought of this when she heard the cries of the merchants over their card games. Finally she decided she must do something about it.

'I'll write to the priest,' she thought. 'He might be able to get them to help me.'

So, sitting down in one of her rare moments of peace and quiet, she wrote a letter to the priest saying how poor she was. She often heard the merchants playing cards, she said, and she was sure more money changed hands in their club in one night than her husband earned in a year. Did the priest think he might be able to help?

When the priest received this letter he looked at it for a long time. Then, making his mind up, he put it carefully in his pocket, and waited until the evening.

That night the card game got going at the merchant's club as usual. A pile of money was spread across the table when there was a knock on the door. Surprised at the interruption, one of the merchants went to the door. He was even more surprised to see the priest standing there.

'Good evening,' said the priest.
'Good evening.'
'I'd like to come and play,' went on the priest.

At this the merchant was so staggered that he could not speak. Wordlessly he waved the priest to a seat at the table.

Once he was in position the priest took the poor woman's letter out of his pocket and laid it in the middle of the table. As he did so he said quietly:

'Hearts are trumps.'

One after the other the merchants read the letter as it was passed from hand to hand. Finally their leader caught the eyes of the others and lifted his eyebrows in an unspoken question. Each of the merchants nodded in turn.

The leader swept all the money on the table into a pile. Then he put it into a bag and handed it to the priest.

'You're right,' he said. 'Hearts are trumps.'

(Adapted from a Jewish folk tale)

Hymn
'I come like a beggar' (*Come and Praise* Vol 2, 90)

Prayer
There are many sayings about money, for example: *Money is the root of all evil. Money makes the world go round. Money makes money.*

Dear God, Help us to appreciate the good things money can do if it is used wisely. Please listen to our prayers when we ask that all men use it wisely.

Amen

The Bible says
The man who loves money can never have enough, and the man who is in love with great wealth enjoys no return from it.

Ecclesiastes 5: 10

Class presentation ideas
This assembly lends itself well to dramatisation. Divide the presenting area into two by a screen. One side of this screen could be used to portray the merchants' club; the other could show the poor woman's home.

'The priest' could be situated at the back of the hall so that the drama moves to and from him as it progresses.

46 The wise vineyard owner

Presenter's note
This is one of those stories where a subterfuge is used to get the right results in the end. It tells how a man thought up a plan to cure his lazy sons – for their own good.

Introduction
This is the story of an old man who had a very successful vineyard which had been built up by his hard work. He also had two lazy sons and he worried about how they would look after the vineyard when he had died.

Core material
An old vineyard owner knew that he was going to die. He had made his vineyard successful by working very hard, but his own sons were lazy.

'I wonder,' thought the old man to himself. 'When I die they won't bother to work the land and everything will be lost – that is unless I can teach them a lesson.'

For a while the old man lay in his bed thinking – then he sent for his two sons. They arrived and sat on either side of his bed. They might have been lazy but they were certainly not unkind.

'Father,' said the eldest,' we wish you were better. How can we help you?'

'Yes, what can we do?' repeated the other.

'You cannot help me my sons,' replied the old man. 'I am old and weary and will die soon. But do not mourn for me because I have had a long and happy life.'

The two sons looked sadly at each other.

'No, I have called you here to help yourselves,' went on the old man. 'You see I am going to tell you about my great treasure.'

'Treasure?' cried the eldest son.

'Treasure?' gasped his brother.

'Yes – treasure,' repeated their father. 'There is a great treasure hidden im my vineyard. When I die you must dig to find it.'

A few days later the old man died. Shortly afterwards the two sons got out some spades and began digging over the land of the vineyard.

Day after day they dig and turned over soil. This went on for weeks and they found no treasure – but the next year the vines produced a rich and wonderful crop of grapes, the best that there had ever been.

(Adapted from an Aesop's fable)

Hymn
'I planted a seed,' (*Come and Praise* Vol 2, 134)

Prayer

Lord – so often we do not know what is good for us. Help us to see the way we should shape our lives, and the way in which we should direct our activities.
Amen

The Bible says

What profit does one get from his labour? I have seen the business that God has given men to keep them busy. He has made everything to suit its time; moreover he has given men a sense of time past and future . . . I know that there is nothing good for man except to be happy and live the best life he can while he is alive.

Ecclesiastes 3: 10–12

Class presentation ideas

Presenters could show a series of pictures linked with 'question and answer' routines which explain them, eg:

Picture 1: The sons digging in the vineyard.
Question Why are these two men digging?
Answer They are the sons of a vineyard owner who has told them that there is treasure buried in his vineyard.

Picture 2: A large question mark.
Question Why has he done that?
Answer Because he is old and he knows that he is going to die. He also knows that his sons are lazy.

Picture 3: The two young men – tired – having dug over the entire vineyard.
Question Did they find the treasure?
Answer Not the sort of treasure they thought they were looking for.

Picture 4: Enormous bunches of grapes.
Question What does this picture mean?
Answer It shows the treasure the two sons got later because they worked so hard in turning over and digging the ground in the vineyard. This was what the old man hoped would happen – and the sons would learn from it.

The assembly could then be 'rounded off' with the hymn, prayer and Bible reading.

47 'I can help him'

Presenter's note
This is about two men trying to help each other, as generously and unobtrusively as possible.

Introduction
Today's story is about two brothers who loved each other very much. Each determined to give the other some secret help . . .

Core material
Isaac looked at his wife and six children as they sat round the table eating their meal.

'What a joy they are,' he thought. 'Poor Abraham, how lonely he must be with no-one but himself. I must try and help him.'

Abraham was Isaac's older brother.

Late that night when it was dark Isaac went out into the barn. The harvest had just been collected and he was certain he could spare a sack of grain for his brother. Hoisting it on his back he carried it through the darkness and left it by a tree just over the boundary on his brother's land.

Earlier that day Abraham had been having a splendid meal in his house.

'I've got all I need for myself,' he thought, 'but my dear brother Isaac who farms next door has all those children to feed. I must try to help him.'

So later that night Abraham got a sack of grain from his harvest and carried it through the night, putting it by a tree just near the boundary on his brother's land.

Early next morning both of the brothers went out to their farms at the same time. Each came to the trees near their boundary lines and saw the sacks.

When they saw them each realised what the other had done. Leaving the sacks where they were they walked towards each other, and wept with joy.

(Adapted from an old Jewish folk tale)

Hymn
'Come my brothers, praise the Lord' (*Come and Praise* Vol 2, 20)

Prayer
Let us give thanks this morning for brothers and sisters; the joy of belonging to a family; the wonder of having someone to care for, and someone to care for us. Let us also think about people who are less fortunate and may be lonely. Please God, help them to find the joy of friendship.

Amen

The Bible says
When you do some act of charity, do not announce it with a flourish of trumpets . . . No, when you do some act of charity, do not let your left hand know what your right is doing: your good deed must be kept secret.

Matthew 6: 3–4

Class presentation ideas

Preparation
Divide the presentation area into two. One half could represent Isaac's home; the other Abraham's.

Development
The presenters act out the scene in each area, following the story. The 'trees' might be at the back of the hall so that the brothers move through the audience to leave their sacks. The denouement could therefore take place at the back of the hall.

Conclusion
Follow-up work could involve kindnesses done by brothers and sisters. Particular emphasis could be put on kindness done unobtrusively.

48 The Feast

Presenter's note
Children have a keen sense of justice and fair play. This old folk tale from the Far East is therefore very satisfying as it leads, step by step, to sharp practice getting its just deserts.

Introduction
You've probably heard the phrase: 'He's too clever for his own good'. You might think of it when you listen to this story of a sly and selfish monkey.

Core material
'Get it out, quickly, get it out.'

The monkey cried out impatiently and pointed to the thorn which was stuck in its tail. Anxious to help, the barber took his razor and cut round the thorn. Inevitably a bit of the monkey's tail was cut.

'How dare you?' screamed the monkey when he saw what had happened. 'How dare you?'

'But . . . began the poor barber, who had only been trying to help.

'You've got a choice,' went on the monkey furiously. 'Either put that piece of tail back or give me your razor.'

The barber looked hopelessly at the small cut on the monkey's tail – and handed over the razor.

Feeling very pleased with himself the monkey set off through the forest on his way home. Before long he came across an old woman cutting wood. She had quite a pile at her feet but was obviously very tired.

The monkey went up to her and held out his razor.

'That looks terribly hard work,' he said. 'Please take this razor to make the job easier.'

The old woman looked at the razor doubtfully, but she thought how kind the monkey was trying to be – and she didn't want to hurt his feelings.

'Well . . . that's very kind of you sir.'

So, taking the razor she set to work to cut a piece of wood with it. Just as she had feared, the razor broke.

'Look at that!' screamed the monkey. 'You've broken my razor deliberately.'

'But . . .' began the old woman.

'Either repair my razor – or give me your whole pile of wood,' exclaimed the monkey nastily.

With a sigh the old woman handed over the wood.

Smugly the monkey went off with his pile of wood, looking for his next victim. It was not long before a delicious smell of cooking wafted through the air. The monkey followed it until he came across a crippled man trying to cook some meat on a tiny wood fire.

'Ha,' said the monkey, 'you'll never cook that unless you have more wood.'

'I've got to do the best I can,' replied the man. 'You see it is very difficult for me to get more wood.'

He pointed to his crippled leg.

'Take mine,' said the monkey. 'That will get the job done much better.'

'Well that's very kind of you. Thank you indeed sir.'

The monkey put the wood on the fire. In a few minutes the meat was deliciously cooked – and all the wood was burnt. Immediately the monkey started to shout and complain.

'You've used all my wood. I've none left! You'll have to pay for that. Give me your meat.'

For a moment the crippled man tried to protest, but the monkey snatched the meat away from him.

'Success,' said the monkey to himself, as he hurried away. 'What a good morning's work!'

Now it so happened that a pack of hungry dogs were also in the forest – and they picked up the scent of the meat. Within minutes they found the monkey, chased him away, and thoroughly enjoyed a spendid meal of the meat.

Hymn
'I planted a seed' (*Come and Praise* Vol 2, 134)

Prayer
Help us, O Lord, never to try and take advantage of other people. Give us the strength of character to try and help those who are less fortunate than ourselves. Teach us always to value fairness.

Amen

The Bible says
Those who rejoice at the downfall of good men will be trapped and consumed with pain.

Ecclesiasticus 27: 29

Class presentation ideas

Preparation
Presenters could draw a series of large pictures portraying the progress of this story. A series of readings appropriate to each picture could then be prepared, and tape recorded.

Development
The assembly could be presented by various children holding up the pictures and then securing them in sequence. At the same time the tape with their commentary would be running related to the story.

Conclusion
Further research might be done in other classrooms to find stories where unworthy deeds get what they deserve.

49 'The Patience of a Saint'

Presenter's note

Some stories emphasise virtues which can be related to other aspects of life. In this instance the virtue is patience, and the story deals with a saint who practised it in the extreme.

Introduction

You may have heard people say, 'Oh, he's got the patience of a saint'. Many people think this saying came about because of the story which follows.

Core material

Lent is the season of the Christian year when Christians think about the mistakes they have made and how their faith can help them live better lives in future. To help with these ideas they often 'give up' things they like during Lent and concentrate more on prayers and suitable thoughts.

Every time the season of Lent came round one Christian, whose name was St Kevin, decided that the best way he could pray and think was to leave the company of all his friends and go and live by himself in an isolated hut.

'Once I'm there I'll be able to think, pray and read,' Kevin said to himself as he took the familiar path through the cool wood to where his cottage stood. After about an hour's journey he reached the tiny simple hut. Pushing open the unlocked door he went in and threw the window wide. Then, kneeling, he began to pray.

Now it was Kevin's custom when he prayed to put his hand out of the window and keep it, palm facing open and upwards towards heaven.

Soon the saint was deep in prayer. Then he felt a movement on his open hand. Opening his eyes he saw that a blackbird had landed on his hand, as if it had come home to its nest. As Kevin watched, the bird laid an egg in the palm of his hand.

'How wonderful,' thought the saint, 'but if I move something terrible might happen.'

So the kind and gentle saint kept his hand in exactly the same position until the young birds were fully hatched.

Hymn

'All the animals' (*Come and Praise* Vol 2, 80)

Prayer

Dear God, Help us to learn the virtue of patience. Help us to be patient when it seems that we will never succeed in something we want, or need, to do. Help us to be patient with other people whose behaviour might annoy or irritate us.

Help us to be patient when our lives are not progressing as we think they ought to.

  We ask for your help.

  Amen

The Bible says
Countless things are made by your hand,
And the earth is full of your creatures.
All of them look to you
To give them food at the proper time.
What you give them they gather up;
When you open your hand they eat their
fill.
May your glory stand forever
And may you rejoice in your works.
                    Adapted from Psalm 104

Class presentation ideas
This is the sort of story which very young children can dramatise successfully for the appreciation and enjoyment of older children. This might be done through a spoken narrative with mimed actions.

50 A practical saint

Presenter's note
This morning's story is about a saint who never hesitated to give positive, practical help.

Introduction
Today's story is about a young man who was captured by pirates and sold as a slave. He later served in a galley and eventually became one of France's most famous saints.

Core material
Vincent was born in France in the late sixteenth century.

'He's not going to be a poor farmer like me,' said his father. 'Certainly not! He's got brains and he must use them.'

Vincent was clever at school and he studied very hard. As a result of this he was able to go to Spain to finish his studies. There he became a priest and then he prepared to go back home to France.

It was on this journey that the first disaster of his life took place. Hardly had his ship put to sea than there was a terrifying shout from the lookout.

'Pirate ship on the port bow!'

In less than an hour Vincent's ship was captured by the Turkish pirates. Then he, and everybody else on the ship were taken to Tunis and sold as slaves.

After being a slave for two masters Vincent finally managed to escape. He made his way back to France again. This time he got there safely and became a village priest near Paris.

Then, however, a rich Frenchman called Gondi asked Vincent to come and teach his children. Vincent agreed, and found that the rich man was in charge of the king's galleys. These were ships which were rowed by dozens of slaves, poor men who were chained to their oars. When their ships were in dock these men were thrown, still chained, into deep dungeons.

Vincent set about helping them. He talked to them and tried to have their conditions made easier. One day one of the galley slaves was ill, so Vincent took his place at the oars. Gondi, the rich Frenchman he worked for, was horrified and astonished when Vincent returned a week later, battered and bleeding after his days chained to the oars in the galley. He then listened to Vincent's pleas and gave him money so that a hospital could be built to care for the galley slaves.

Next Vincent set about helping the thousands of desparately poor orphan children who roamed the streets of Paris. He began by asking all Gondi's rich friends if they would give him money to help. When he got this money he built hospitals and then began to train priests to work with these homeless children.

He even managed to persuade many rich ladies to leave their comfortable homes and give help too.

Vincent became one of the most famous men in France and he is particularly remembered on July 19th. He died in 1660.

Hymn
'Break Out' (*Come and Praise* Vol 2, 91)

Prayer
Let us give thanks this morning for those who inspire us with their bravery, encourage us with their determination and kindness, help us with their skill, patience and thoughtfulness.

    Amen

The Bible says
'*When you do some act of charity, do not let your left hand know what your right is doing; your good deed must be secret.*'

Matthew 6: 3–4

Class presentation ideas
This is an excellent subject for a 'This is your life' assembly. Obviously Vincent would be the central figure. People who 'knew' him could be: his father; a fellow scholar; a reformed member of the pirate crew who captured him; a fellow slave; one of his parishioners near Paris; Gondi; the slave he sat next to on the galley; a Paris orphan.

51 A forgiving father

Presenter's note
Despite its familiarity, this story has considerable impact on children. This is particularly so in the context of a 'fairness and forgiveness' theme.

Introduction
Forgiving people is not easy. Perhaps most difficult of all is to forgive somebody who you care about very deeply, and who has let you down. This morning's story is about this kind of forgiveness.

Core material
'Fed up!' said the young man. 'Fed up – that's what I am.'

His older brother sighed. He had heard all this before. Some people seemed to do nothing but complain.

A little while later the younger brother stood before his father, who was a well-off farmer.

'Look here, father,' he said. 'When you die your money will be shared out between Joseph and me. Well, I don't want to stay here anymore, I'm fed up. Can I have my share of the money now to spend it how I choose?'

The farmer was sad and disappointed to hear his son talk in this way. He needed his young son to help work the farm and he was upset at his selfishness. But he agreed.

'Very well my boy,' he said, 'if that is what you really want I'll get the money ready for you.'

A few days later John, the yonger son, was bidding his father and brother a casual farewell and preparing to leave the country.

'I'll soon be away from this dull place,' he thought. Then I'll be able to enjoy life.'

It soon seemed as if John was right. When he reached another land he had plenty of money, and he soon found plenty of people to help him enjoy spending it. He did no work and the days went by quickly as he and his friends ate the best of food and drank fine wine. Then, one day, the young man found he had no money left.

'That won't matter,' he thought. 'I'm sure my friends have some. It'll just be their turn to spend it now.'

Then he got a shock. Without his money his so-called friends weren't interested in him one little bit. Now he was just a lonely stranger in a foreign land. He would have to get a job.

Now at this time there was a famine in the land and food was very expensive. The best job that John could get was looking after pigs. His wages were pitifully low.

One day he stood looking at the pigs in his care. His clothes were by now in rags and he couldn't afford any more. He was desperately hungry and as he stood there he realised that he was even hungry enough to eat the swill the pigs were grunting and pushing over.

'That's dreadful,' he said to himself. 'What an absolute fool I've been. On my father's farm even the poorest of servants has good, clean clothes and plenty to eat. I wonder . . .'

John decided he would go home. He no longer felt fit to be called his father's son but he would ask if he could work as a servant. He set off on the long journey home.

When John was still a long way, off, his father, who happened to be outside the farmhouse, saw him coming. The old man ran to meet him, weeping with joy.

'How can I say how sorry I am, father?' said John. 'I'm not worthy to be your son anymore but please let me be one of your servants.'

The farmer would not hear of it. He got out fine clothes for his son, gave him shoes and a ring and told his servants to prepare a special meal.

When Joseph, the elder brother, heard about this he was angry. After all when John left he had had to work doubly hard – and now all this fuss was being made over the brother who had left him in the lurch!

When he got home however, Joseph saw his father's joy.

'Joseph,' said the old man, 'all I have is yours, but help me welcome your brother back. I thought he was lost but he is found again.'

When Joseph realised how happy his father was he couldn't be angry any more. The family celebrated being together once again.

(from Luke 15: 11–32)

Hymn
'Somebody greater' (*Come and Praise* Vol 1, 5)

Prayer
Dear God, we ask you to forgive us for our many faults – our thoughtlessness, our unkindness, our laziness, our selfishness. Help us never to judge other people when we need so much forgiveness ourselves.

Amen

The Bible says
If your brother wrongs you, reprove him; and if he repents forgive him. Even if he wrongs you seven times in a day and comes back to you seven times saying, 'I'm sorry,' you are to forgive him.

Luke 17:4

Class presentation ideas

This is one of those Biblical stories which is 'tailor made' for acting by the children. A few simple costumes would heighten the effect and the action could be guided and held together by a narrator.

52 A family reunited

Presenter's note
This story of Joseph and his brothers is one of forgiveness and compassion (see *Genesis* 37–46).

Introduction
This story is about a family. There was a great deal of jealousy amongst the brothers of this family and they did a terrible thing to the second youngest, who was called Joseph. Later Joseph had a chance to pay them back for their cruelty and jealousy. Listen to what happened.

Core material
Once there was a family of 12 brothers. They lived in a country called Canaan, with their father, Jacob. Of all the brothers, Joseph was his father's favourite. The others were very jealous of him. One day they were all out in the desert with their sheep. The brothers attacked Joseph and threw him into a pit. Then they saw some foreign traders and they sold Joseph to them, as a slave. When they got home, they told their father that Joseph was dead.

However Joseph survived and became a very important man in Egypt.

Years later the crops began to fail in Canaan.

'If we don't do something about it,' said Jacob, 'we will starve. You'd better go to Egypt and see if you can get some sacks of corn there. Benjamin, my youngest son will stay here with me. I remember what happened before and I don't want to lose another son like I lost Joseph.'

So the brothers set out on the long journey to Egypt. When they got there they were taken to see Joseph, who was now the second most important man in the country. He looked at the group of tired, dusty, hungry men – and he recognised them instantly. His brothers! That very same group of men who had sold him as a slave to a caravan of merchants all that time ago. Joseph felt a surge of anger sweep over him, but he managed to keep his face stern and unwavering.

'Sir,' said Reuben, the eldest brother. 'Our family is starving. Can you help us.'

Joseph then realised that none of his brothers had recognised him!

'We don't help spies,' he said coldly.

'But we are not spies,' gasped Reuben. 'We are ten brothers – and our father and youngest brother are at home in Canaan.'

'Very well,' replied Joseph, 'but I want to be sure you are telling the truth – so you will leave one brother behind, and when you return for more corn you will bring your youngest brother back here with you.'

Joseph then snapped his fingers and his servants began to fill sacks of corn for the brothers. Simeon, one of them, was taken away and put in prison until they returned.

Some days later Jacob welcomed back his sons. He was worried when he heard their story. Then he got another shock – when the sacks of corn were opened the money to pay for it was found inside.

'We will have to deal with this man again,' said Jacob, 'but when we do, take twice as much money to pay for the corn. And I suppose Benjamin will have to go with you.'

Sure enough the corn soon disappeared and the need for more grew desperate. Once more the brothers journeyed to Egypt, and stood before Joseph. This time, to their surprise, he was much more friendly. He arranged a splendid meal for them at his palace.

Whilst this was going on he organised the filling of their sacks. And he instructed his servants to hide a silver goblet from his palace in Benjamin's sack.

Next morning the brothers sat off for home. They had not gone very far when shouts from behind made them stop. A group of heavily-armed Egyptian soldiers soon surrounded them.

'We have reason to believe you are thieves,' exclaimed the officer. 'Open those sacks.'

'Gladly,' said Reuben, 'we have nothing to hide.'

Then, to his horror, the silver goblet came tumbling out of Benjamin's sack!

'So,' cried the officer, 'don't waste your breath trying to explain this – round them up, men!'

Some hours later the desperate brothers stood yet again before Joseph.

'This is how you repay my kindness!' he shouted. 'Thieves . . . you will be punished. Take the one whose sack contained the goblet and throw him in prison.'

'No!' cried Reuben, 'not Benjamin. Although we are all innocent punish us if you will, but not Benjamin. If he does not return it will kill our father.'

In his desperation, he began to tell the whole story of what they had done on that sad occasion years ago. Suddenly Joseph put up his hand.

'Stop,' he said quietly. 'You do not need to tell me that story because I know it. I am your brother Joseph.'

The brothers gasped. Could it be true? Then, worry and fear etched themselves even more strongly on their faces. Now there was no hope. They would surely die for their wrongdoing.

'Come round me,' ordered Joseph. 'Once I was angry and would have punished you all. But as you see, things have worked out well for me. Go, and bring our father back here so that we can be together again.'

This was done and the Egyptian ruler allowed Joseph's whole family to live in plenty with him in Egypt.

Hymn
'I listen and I listen' (*Come and Praise* Vol 1, 60)

Prayer
Lord, free us from jealousy and envy. Help us to be content and satisfied. Free us from bitter words and actions. Help us to live with warmth and concern in our hearts.
  Amen

The Bible says
Envy and anger shorten a man's life, and anxiety brings premature old age.
Ecclesiasticus 30: 24

Class presentation ideas
In this case the core material might form the conclusion of the assembly. Prior to it the presenters could, in various groups, act out a few short plays which focus on the strengths needed to forgive.

These could start with very elementary situations within the children's own experience – the broken window, the missing cake, the favourite toy broken by a friend etc.

Once the core material has been reached more could be made of the first part for dramatic purposes – Joseph's 'technicolour dreamcoat' is a memorable feature for children.

53 The three hundred

Presenter's note

The moral of this Bible story is 'do not be discouraged by apparently insurmountable difficulties (see *Judges* 6.8).

Introduction

Sometimes in life difficulties seem so enormous that they are impossible to overcome. This morning's story describes a situation which begins like this. The Israelites were desperate – a larger, stronger army was making their lives impossible. Listen to what happened.

Core material

'It's no good, we can't do anything about it.'

'But it is desperate.'

'If only there was somebody to take charge.'

So grumbled the Israelites on their farms and in their villages. They were complaining about the terrifying raids of the Midianites. Regularly these raiders swept into the attack on their long-striding camels, spreading death and destruction in their path.

One day, after such a raid, a young man called Gideon stepped outside his home in the Jezreel valley. He saw a stranger standing there. 'If we are God's people, why doesn't he do something about these raids?' said Gideon to the stranger.

'He's going to,' replied the stranger, 'with your help.'

'My help?' gasped Gideon, 'but I'm just the youngest son of a very poor family.'

Nevertheless, with the stranger's encouragement, Gideon set about organising an army. The Midianites heard about this and, getting together thousands of men, got ready to destroy the Israelites. Then God spoke to Gideon.

'You've got too many men.'

'But the Midianites have got thousands more . . .' protested Gideon.

'Listen,' said God, 'send home all your men who are frightened and take the rest down to the river to drink.'

When the soldiers heard they could go home if they were frightened they left in their hundreds. As instructed, Gideon took the rest to drink at the river.

When they got there some of the Israelites lay at the water's edge and drank. Others were more cautious, scooped up water to drink but kept their eyes open for possible danger.

'Keep only those who were cautious,' said God.

Gideon sent the rest home and was left with an army of only three hundred men.

'How can we win with so few men?' wondered Gideon, but he was already being made aware of a shrewd plan.

That night Gideon and his three hundred men crept through the darkness towards the Midianite camp. Each carried a sword, a trumpet and a candle inside a pot. The Midianite camp was still and quiet, even the sentries dozed, thinking there was so little to fear from the Israelites.

Suddenly the silence of the night was broken by hundreds of trumpet blasts. Immediately afterwards there was a great crashing as the Israelites' pots were broken and dozens of flickering candles sprang up all round the Midianite camp.

With shouts of terror the Midianites leapt up, startled and awake.

'We're being attacked!'

'There are thousands of them.'

'We're surrounded!'

'Run . . . run for your lives!'

Then the Israelite trumpets sounded again, followed by shouts of, 'For God and Gideon!'

By now the Midianite camp was in total panic. Fleeing soldiers tore down their tents, terrified camels ran in all directions. Thousands of men were in full retreat.

The three hundred Israelites had won a great and painless victory. Now Gideon could go home again and live in peace.

Hymn
'Come my brothers praise the Lord' (*Come and Praise* Vol 1, 20)

Prayer
Dear God, Give us faith to persist when everything seems against us; give us the will and determination not to give in; give us the words to ask for your help and guidance.

Amen

The Bible says
In dealing with men it is God's purposes to test them and to see what they truly are . . . Fear God and obey his commandments; there is no more to man than this. For God brings everythings we do to judgement.

Ecclesiastes 3:18; 12:13

Class presentation ideas
An apparently 'ad libbed' and spontaneous response from the presenters

could be most effective here. (In fact the ad-libbed approach will have been carefully planned, of course.)

Play some rousing martial music as presenters and audience enter the hall. The presenters could then stand in two groups, chatting and milling around. One of the groups could be Midianite soliders, the others Israelite soldiers. A speaker could then begin:

Speaker Good morning everybody. Today we are fortunate because one of our reporters has been able to gather together some of the soldiers who were involved in the famous battle between three hundred Israelite soliders, and the great Midianite army. Here he (or she) is . . .

Having introduced the 'reporter' the Speaker could retreat, leaving the way for the reporter to take over.

Reporter This morning I am going to speak to some of the Israelite and Midianite soldiers who were involved in this great event. First however I would like to give you the background to the story . . .

This will provide an opportunity for a speaker to fill in the background to the attack.

Once this has been done the reporter moves to the Midianite group and interviews several of them to draw forth the information that they thought they had been defeated by a vastly superior force.

The reporter then moves to the Israelites. Gradually, in response to his questions, the truth of what actually happened is revealed.

54 Help when needed

Presenter's note

This Bible story of Rahab saving the lives of two Israelites emphasises how often we receive help from the most unexpected quarters. (see *Joshua* 2: 1–24).

Introduction

We never know when we are going to need help. This morning's story is about two Israelites who found themselves in great danger. They were helped by a woman who might have been thought of as an enemy. She risked her own life to help them.

Core material

The two men walked round the city walls. They were surprised to see a house built into the walls, with a window looking out beyond the city.

'Strange place, Jericho,' said one of the men.

'Yes,' said the other, 'when we get back we can report to Joshua exactly how things are here.'

Just at that moment a woman appeared in the doorway of the house built into the wall.

'Welcome,' she said to the two strangers. 'I noticed you looking at my house, would you like to see inside?'

The two men thanked Rahab, for that was the woman's name, and went inside. No sooner had they done so than a commotion broke out in the street. Rahab looked out and then beckoned to the two men urgently.

'There are soldiers everywhere,' she said, 'quick, out through the window and onto the roof. There's some flax drying up there. Cover yourselves with it and keep absolutely still and quiet.'

Within minutes soliders burst into Rahab's house.

'Where are they?' cried their officer. 'They were seen to come in here.'

'Who?' asked Rahab.

'Those Israelite spies, woman. You know who I men!'

'Oh – I asked two visitors to the city to come in because they were looking at my house. Anyway, they left a few minutes ago. They went that way.'

Rahab pointed out of the window towards the distant Israelite camp.

'Right, come on men, let's get after them,' shouted the officer, and the soldiers clattered noisily out.

On the roof the two Israelites lay motionless. They had heard everything. A few minutes later a knocking on the bottom of the roof told them it was safe to come down.

'Why did you to that for us?' one of them asked Rahab.

'Well you were visitors to my house, and I knew at once that you were

Israelites. Everybody has heard about your people's escape from Egypt, and I have thought a lot about your God.'

'You have saved our lives by your kindness and courage, Rahab,' said the other man. 'Your help will be rewarded.'

'Yes,' went on his friend. 'When the Israelites come, get all your family in this house and then hang a red cloth out of the window. We will make sure you are all safe.'

Shortly afterwards, when it was dark, the two Israelites slid down a rope of sheets from Rahab's window. As they made their way back to camp they thought of the woman who had given them help when it was most desperately needed.

Hymn
'One more step' (*Come and Praise* Vol 1, 47).

Prayer
O Lord teach us to be caring, thoughtful people, because only then can we appreciate the needs of others. Help us to be kind in thought, word and deed, and to treat others as we would wish to be treated ourselves.

Amen

The Bible says
'Is there a man among you who will offer his son a stone when he asks for bread, or a snake when he asks for fish? . . . always treat others as you would like them to treat you.'

Matthew 7: 9–12

Class presentation ideas

Preparation
In advance, the presenting groups should prepare a series of large pictures depicting the events of the story. These might show: the houses in the walls of the city of Jericho; the two Israelites; Rahab; the commander of the soldiers; the house search; 'hiding on the roof'; the escape down the rope of sheets; the red cloth.

Several groups within the class could be responsible for a picture each, and a short written commentary about it.

Development
On the morning of the assembly, groups could take their places with covered up pictures and commentaries to hand. Then pictures are revealed, one by one with appropriate comment, until the story is told.

55 David and Jonathan

Presenter's note
This story of David and Jonathan emphasises that we often need practical help in difficult situations (see *1 Samuel* 20: 1–42)

Introduction
So often in life we intend to do a good deed but don't get round to it. In this story a young man sees that his friend urgently needs help, and he does something about it straight away.

Core material
There was once a king called Saul. He was a very moody man and people never quite knew what sort of a temper he would be in.

One day Saul was feeling perticularly miserable. So he sent for David, his son Jonathan's best friend, to play the harp for him. David often played beautiful music for Saul but on this occasion the king was in a violent mood. Displeased with something David had done, Saul tried to kill him with a spear. David fled into the countryside. A little while later Jonathan met him there.

'I'm so sorry about this,' said Jonathan, 'I wish I could say it was safe for you to come back.'

'So do I,' replied David. 'Without your help I'd probably be dead already.'

'I'll have one more try to get my father to see sense,' said Jonathan, 'but he must not find out where you are.'

'Thank you,' said David.

'This is what I'll do,' went on Jonathan. 'Tomorrow I'll come out here with a servant. I'll fire three arrows as if I was aiming at something. If I shout to the servant; 'Look, the arrows are on this side,' that means all is well and we can go back together. If I shout, 'Look, the arrows are on the other side and further on,' that means my father is determined to kill you and you cannot ever return.'

David was worried when he heard this and went back into hiding when his friend had gone. He knew that Jonathan was taking a great risk for him – Saul was a very dangerous man to cross.

The next day David crouched behind a rock as Jonathan and his servant appeared. David hoped desperately that everything would be all right. Suddenly one, two, three arrows curved up into the air.

'Look,' shouted Jonathan, 'the arrows are on the other side and further on.'

David heard the shout with great sadness. He remained in hiding until Jonathan's servant had collected the arrows and was sent back to the city.

Then he came out from behind the rock and clasped his best friend.
　'It's no good?' he asked.
　'I'm afraid you'll never be safe if you return,' answered Jonathan.
　So the two friends parted, for ever.

Hymn
'The Sharing Bread' (*Come and Praise* Vol 2, 139)

Prayer
Dear God,
Help us to take action when we know we should – even if we are not sure that
the action is going to succeed. Don't let us waste our talents or let our good
deeds and thoughful actions lie hidden under a stone.
　Amen

The Bible says
'*A faithful friend is a secure shelter*'

Ecclesiasticus 6:14

Class presentation ideas

Preparation
Prepare one or two 'newspaper placards' with messages like: DAVID IN
HIDING! REWARD FOR FINDING HARPIST! KING SEEKS SON'S
FRIEND. Placed these in the hall or on the way to it so that the audience can
see them.
　The assembly could begin with a 'question and answer' routine:

Speaker 1　What are the newspaper placards about?
Speaker 2　They are about a missing man.
Speaker 1　Why was he missing? What had he done?
Speaker 2　He had done nothing – listen to this story.

The core material could then be presented in narrative and/or dramatised
form.

56 A time to sing and dance

Presenter's note
This is a story of joy and celebration – a chance for everybody to enjoy themselves (see *2 Samuel* 6: 12–22)

Introduction
There are moments in our lives when we should all celebrate and enjoy ourselves. Birthdays, Christmas, weddings, the return of friends or relatives – all these are times of great happiness and joy.

This morning's story tells us of a great day in the story of the Israelites, and how it provided an opportunity to celebrate for everyone – from the king to the humblest of the people.

Core material
When the Israelites settled in Jerusalem it was a great moment for them. Before the city was built there, Abraham had walked on this hill. In the distance was the great desert which had been crossed.

'Jerusalem will be our holy city,' said King David. 'To make sure that it is, we will have the Ark of the Covenant brought in through the gates. It will be the greatest celebration we have ever know.'

The Ark was the Israelites' most precious, holy possession. It was being kept in a barn some distance from the city. David set about organising things. Dozens of men went out to the barn to fetch the Ark. They placed it in a cart drawn by oxen. Priests led the way back to the city and as the procession moved along people sang and danced with joy.

Soon the city gates came into sight and a great roar went up. Thousands of Israelites were lining the streets waiting for the marvellous moment when the Ark came through the gates to its final resting place.

Slowly the procession passed through the gates. At its head went King David, dancing joyfully. Everybody who wasn't dancing and singing seemed to be blowing a trumpet or clashing a pair of cymbals. It was a fantastic moment.

Eventually the Ark reached the special tent which had been put up to receive it. Then a huge feast was held. Again King David was to be seen everywhere, handing round sweets and food and laughing with pleasure.

At last the celebrations ended and a tired and happy king made his way back to the palace. There he met a young princess called Michal.

'That was disgusting,' she said, 'you – a – king – dancing and singing and handing round food.'

For a moment David was silent. Then, reaching out to take the princess's arm, he spoke quietly.

'Today is one of the most special days in our people's history,' he said. 'It is the day our ancestors longed for, when the wanderings in the desert have stopped and the Ark has come home to our holy city of Jerusalem. Worshipping God does not mean that man should be miserable – there are times when we should celebrate – and enjoy great moments in the best way we possibly can.'

Hymn
'Fill your hearts with joy and gladness,' (*Come and Praise* Vol 1, 9).

Prayer
Dear God, We thank you for those special moments of fun and laughter, of music and dancing, of happiness and joy. Thank you for giving us pleasure in this way. Please help those people who, for whatever reason, find it difficult to laugh and share in celebrations.
    Amen

The Bible says
I know that there is nothing good for man except to be happy and live the best life he can while he is alive. Moreover, that a man should eat and drink and enjoy himself, in return for all his labours, is a gift of God. A merry heart keeps a man alive, and joy lengthens the span of his days.
Ecclesiastes 3: 12–14; 30:22

Class presentation ideas
A very simple, symbolic 'Ark' could be made, and a number of musical instruments – percussion, recorders – collected before the assembly. A little pre-assembly rehearsal would be useful, so that the presenters know exactly where they come in the procession, and what they have to do. However, a feeling of spontaneity is important.
    The main feature of the class presentation would be the procession, involving all the presenters. This should be done with a maximum of controlled noise and gaiety, with plenty of clapping and playing of instruments. The procession comes through the audience into its position in the hall, then stops whilst a reader explains:

Reader   When King David brought the Ark of the Convenant into Jerusalem it was a great moment. It was the day the Israelites had waited for. Now they could worship God in the holy city.

Following the reading there could be more celebrations followed by the little side drama of Michal's confrontation with David.

Conclusion
Hymn, prayer and Bible reading suggestions could make an appropriate conclusion to this assembly.

57 A brilliant decision

Presenter's note
This well-known story about Solomon's wisdom can be a useful starting point to help children to reflect on some of their own experiences (see 1 Kings 3: 16–28).

Introduction
Sometimes we have difficult decisions to make. How do we make them? Where do we get our wisdom or guidance from? Listen to this story of a very wise decision.

Core material
When King Solomon was a young man he wanted to impress his people. In his prayers he asked that he might be given widsom in order to do this. In a very short while his opportunity came about.

'Your majesty,' said the minister, 'we have a very difficult case for your judgement.'

'Indeed,' replied the king, 'tell me about it.'

'We have two women outside,' went on the minister, 'and one baby. Both claim it is theirs.'

'Show them in to me,' ordered Solomon.

A minute later the two women stood before him. One of them clutched a baby tightly to her.

'Now,' said the king calmly, pointing to one of the women, 'tell me your story.'

'Your majesty, when my baby was asleep during the night, this woman exchanged it for her own baby which had died.'

'That's not true, your majesty,' gasped the accused woman, 'this baby is mine.'

Solomon paused.

'It is a very sad story all together. There seems to be only one solution. Guard – your sword.'

'What?'

Solomon nodded towards the guard.

'He will cut the child in two so that you can share.'

Before he could finish the sentence the real mother let out a cry of anguish.

'No . . . no! Give it to her, but don't kill my baby, please . . . please!'

Solomon waved the guard away.

'I think we now know who the real mother is,' he said to his minister.

(1 Kings 3: 16–28)

Hymn
'Make us worthy Lord' (*Come and Praise* Vol 2, 94)

Prayer
Dear God, Teach us to be grateful for the gifts we have been given. Help us to use them as fully as we can for the good of all those with whom we come into contact. Help us to make decisions which are based on truth, honesty and wisdom.

   Amen.

The Bible says
When a man has been given much, much will be expected of him; and the more a man has entrusted to him the more he will be required to pay.

Luke 12:48

Class presentation ideas
The core material, prayer and Biblical reference could form the first part of the assembly, which might then move on to more specific considerations in the second part.

   The theme that, 'from someone who is given a lot, a lot is expected' might be developed using examples from the children's own experience, eg

a)   The 'top' of the school. Children at the top of the school enjoy privileges and prestige. As a consequence they could be expected to set an example for others to follow.
b)   Having been given an environment in which to learn, we should do our best to keep it clean, attractive, pleasant, litter-free etc.
c)   Having been granted good health, adequate food, leisure time, facilities etc we should do something constructive to help the less fortunate.
d)   Having been given the opportunity to acquire 'wisdom' we should work hard to ensure that we do.
e)   Being part of a class and school family we should take our responsibilities seriously and behave towards others as we would like them to behave towards us.

58 The men who owed money

Presenter's note

The story of the debtors from St Matthew's gospel is simple and straight-forward and very effective. This adaptation might be useful for dramatic work with all age groups (see Matthew 18: 23–24).

Introduction

'If only' are two words we often use. 'If only' everybody would behave towards us as we would like them to. In this morning's story a man is allowed to forget about a lot of money he owed. 'If only' he could have behaved as well to someone who owed him a much smaller amount.

Core material

'I need to collect my debts,' said the king. 'Now let me see, who owes me the most?'

'No doubt about that, your majesty,' replied the Chief Minister. 'It is Lord Erring, he has got terrific debts.'

'Inform him that I want my money by the end of the week,' said the king.

Two days later Lord Erring stood before the king.

'Your majesty, I have received your message to pay you the money I owe you. I'm afraid my farms are doing extremely badly at the moment and I'm afraid that I need more time to pay.'

'Very well,' said the king. 'I'll give you another week.'

In a week's time Lord Erring stood again before a rather impatient king.

'I'm sorry, your majesty, I still haven't the money, you see . . .'

'Excuses, excuses!' shouted the king. 'Minister, see that this man's lands are taken at once. Throw his wife and children out of their house and sell it to raise money.'

'No, no. Your majesty, please. Not my family . . . please.'

Now the king was a fair and kind man. He saw how distressed Lord Erring was about his family.

'Hmmm, I would be worried too, if that was happening to my family,' he thought to himself.

Aloud, he said, 'Well, perhaps I don't need the money from you as badly as I thought. Consider the debt wiped out – now go home to your wife and children, give them the good news, and get your affairs in order.'

'Oh thank you, your majesty,' gasped Lord Erring. 'I can never thank you enough for your kindness. Thank you again sir.'

Lord Erring then set out for his home. He hadn't gone very far before he saw a man who had once been a friend of his, and who owed him a small sum of money.

'Hey!' Lord Erring called out. 'I'm glad I've seen you. You owe me £5 – and I want it now.'

'Ah,' said the man. 'I can't give it to you at this moment. Can you give me until tomorrow night and I will bring it round for you. I'll even pay some interest if you will let me have just this extra day to repay you.'

'I certainly will not,' snarled Lord Erring. 'I know your type, trying to dodge out of paying. I want it now!'

So saying, he grabbed hold of the other man, shouting angrily as he did so.

Now unfortunately for Lord Erring, the king's Chief Minister had seen, and heard, all that had gone on. At once he had Lord Erring arrested and brought back before the king.

'You scoundrel,' exclaimed the king when he heard the story. 'I was prepared to let you off a huge sum – and that is how you behaved over a few pounds. You will go straight to prison until your debt is paid in full.'

Hymn
'I listen and I listen,' (*Come and Praise* Vol 1, 60)

Prayer
Dear God, Help us to learn from good examples; from our own mistakes; from stories which guide our thoughts. Keep us learning for the whole of our lives.

Amen

The Bible says
Each man should examine his own conduct for himself; that he can measure his achievement by comparing himself with himself and not with anyone else.

Galatians 6:4

Class presentation ideas
This story has good potential for dramatisation and it could be approached in a fairly structured way. One of the presenters might be introduced to the audience as a reporter who can explore both 'Time' and 'Space' in order to present *Lessons from the Past*.

The reporter can then be transported back to the time of the story's events. As they are acted out he could comment on them and act as a liaison officer between players and audience. This would enable questions to be asked and opinions to be sought from the audience. In this way participation and involvement will hopefully spread to all the children in the hall.

59 The sower and the seeds

Presenter's note
This story of the sower and the seeds is about essentials – in starting and developing life (see Matthew 13: 4–9).

Introduction
Nothing 'just grows'. Whatever it is, the conditions when it is planted must be right, and as life develops it needs to be cared for in different ways. This clearly applies to plants but it applies to people too.

Core material
Jesus often told people stories. These stories often made them think about their own lives. Many people wanted to hear these stories and huge crowds gathered to hear them. Once, the crowds were so big that Jesus had to go out in a boat and then speak to all the people who were listening on the shore.

This is one of the stories he told.

Once there was a man whose job was to plant seeds to make crops grow. As he went about his job a flock of birds flew overhead. Some of the seeds had hardly reached the ground before the birds ate them.

Some more of the seeds landed on rocky ground. The sun shone on them but when they tried to put roots down to get water from the ground they couldn't, because of the rocks. So these seeds died.

Other seeds landed well away from the rocks, but on parts of the earth where there were a lot of weeds. The weeds were already strong and they stopped these seeds from growing.

Some of the seeds however, landed on good soil. The sun shone on them, they sank down roots for water and soon they grew into fine crops.

Hymn
'I planted a seed' (*Come and Praise* Vol 2, 134)

Prayer
Dear God, Help us to appreciate all that is good in the world. Give us the strength to cope with disappointments and setbacks. Help us to make the very best use of what talents we are given.

Amen

The Bible says
There is nothing new under the sun.
$\qquad$ Ecclesiastes 1:9

Class presentation ideas

This assembly could be developed by using the 'question/answer' technique.

One of the presenters asks the audience to listen to a story Jesus told. One of the children then reads 'The sower and the seeds'. In the Question/Answer session, responses could be given by individual children, or a chorus.

Question   Do you think people are like seeds?
Answer   Yes we do.
Question   Why is that?
Answer   People, like seeds, need to start in 'good ground'
Question   How do you mean?
Answer   Babies need conditions which enable them to have proper food, rest and warmth. They need to have these things regularly and they need adults to see that they get them.
Question   How else are people like seeds?
Answer   Both need to be cared for. The sower doesn't throw his seeds anywhere, and parents think a lot about caring properly for their children.
Question   How are people not like seeds?
Answer   Growing children need more than food, light, warmth, exercise. They also need love, friendship, interest, advice.

This could then be developed along various lines:

- drawing a parallel between the 'sower' and Third World countries, and what we can do to help.
- concentrating on individuals within the class, their opinions, personal experiences about care, growth, love etc. in their own lives.
- focusing on the 'message' of the story, linked with other messages in the stories which Jesus told.

60 Into the unknown

Presenter's note
After the ascension of Jesus the early Christians had a very difficult time. Hounded, imprisoned, executed, their lives in Jerusalem became almost impossible. But they refused to give up their beliefs – as this story of Philip shows (see *Acts* 8: 1–25).

Introduction
Most of us don't like going anywhere by ourselves. We prefer to go with our family or friends. Imagine the courage you would need to go to a foreign country by yourself, when travel was difficult and dangerous and the country belonged to your enemies. This morning's story is about a man who did this.

Core material
The group of men stood at the foot of a steep, dusty mountain road. The sun blazed down mercilessly on them and all could have done with a good meal and a long drink.

'You can't be serious,' said one of the men, whose eyes were dark with tiredness.

'I am,' replied another, who seemed less depressed than his companions.

'Look at it this way,' he went on. 'In Jerusalem our lives are worth nothing. Out here in other towns and villages we can tell people about Jesus without such fear of capture and imprisonment. In somewhere like Samaria it will be even better – more people will be willing to listen and learn.'

'But Samaria has always been our enemy.'

'How do you know they won't kill you before you can speak to them?'

'Listen, listen my friends,' said Philip, the man who wanted to go to Samaria, 'our Lord told us to spread the message far and wide – and that is just what I am going to do.'

With a wave of his hand he drove his staff into the hard ground and began to walk to the distant border between Judea and Samaria.

Hours later Philip reached his destination. There he got a surprise. The Samaritans, traditional enemies of his people, welcomed him with kindness and listened carefully to what he had to say. The marvellous story of Jesus had already reached their country and they wanted to hear more about it.

'I can tell you,' said Philip, 'for our Lord wants people like me to spread the good news as far and wide as possible.'

Before long there were many Christians in Samaria. Word of Philip's success spread back to Judea and Peter and John prepared to make the journey to give what help they could.

'You've got to hand it to Philip,' said Peter. 'Not many men would have the courage, and faith, to journey alone into an enemy country as he has done.'

'You're right,' replied John. 'Now the good news is really spreading.'

Hymn

'You shall go out with joy' (*Come and Praise* Vol 2, 98)

Prayer

> Do all the good you can,
> By all the means you can,
> In all the ways you can,
> In all the places you can,
> At all the times you can,
> To all the people you can,
> As long as ever you can.

John Wesley

The Bible says

Let us now sing the praises of famous men . . . some held sway over kingdoms . . . others were sage counsellors.

Ecclesiasticus 44: 1–4

Class presentation ideas

This assembly could be presented by a series of letter readings. Using the core material as the basis for these a number of presenting children could read 'letters' from such people as:

- a Christian being persecuted in Jerusalem
- a soldier charged with helping to get rid of Christians
- somebody who heard Philip talking of going to Samaria
- a Samaritan, after he or she had met Philip
- a person who was writing to Peter to tell him what was happening
- Peter writing to Philip to tell him that he and John were coming to Samaria
- John writing back to Philip after the visit.

Should the teacher feel it would enhance the assembly then one or two of these 'letters' might be supplemented with some appropriate drama.

SECTION B
Plays for assemblies

On an oil rig

Theme Harvest

Calendar location September/October

Preparation
The following 'aids' need to be prepared in advance:

- a tape-recording of sounds suggesting noises heard on an oil rig: howling wind, crashing waves, machinery and equipment being operated, men shouting, a distant helicopter.
- a simple cut-out cardboard figure of an oil rig worker – Ed (life-size if possible)

Pupils will need to rehearse choral speaking.

Part 1
As the presenters and audience move into the hall play the previously prepared tape.

Once everybody is in position, fade out the tape and bring the life-size model of 'Ed' to the front of the presenting area.

Speaker	Today I would like to introduce you to Ed and tell you something about him.
Questioner	Who is Ed then?
Speaker	He's a roustabout.
Questioner	What's that?
Speaker	It means that he is a worker on an off-shore oil rig which drills in the sea for oil. Roustabouts are odd-job-men on oil rigs. They scrape off rust wherever it forms; they paint the rig and wash the decks.
Questioner	How long does Ed work?
Speaker	He works two weeks on the rig and then he is flown away by helicopter to have two weeks off. He works twelve hours every day he is on the rig.

Questioner	That's a lot. What does he do in his hours off?
Speaker	There's not much he can do. He eats and sleeps, of course. Apart from that he might read, play cards, or watch films and TV.
Questioner	What other people work on this oil rig?
Speaker	There's a man called a tool pusher who is in charge of the drilling for oil. He is helped by men called drillers and rotary helpers. There are also engineers, divers, radio operators, geologists, crane drivers, electricians and cooks. As many as 200 men might live on an oil rig.
Questioner	Why do they need to be there at all?
Speaker	Because human beings need to harvest the world's oil supply. We use oil for heat, lubrication, cleaning, most forms of transport. It is also used a lot by industry: for cosmetics, agriculture, textiles, construction, printing and many others. Oil is one of the most important things the earth gives us.
Questioner	What's being on an oil rig like?
Speaker	Often it's very unpleasant. The oil rig is cut off from the rest of the world – its only links are via the radio and the helicopter service. Work on the platform is always dangerous, and in winter the weather is often very bad with freezing winds sweeping over the platform and

huge waves crashing against it. Added to this the work is dirty and exhausting and the constant noise of wind, waves, machinery and pumps is very tiring. Then there are the smells – of oil, of the special mud which is pumped down the drill strings and of the fumes from the diesel generators.

Questioner   The harvest these men work on is a very hard one isn't it?

Speaker   Very hard indeed.

Part 2

The poem below conveys something of life on an oil rig. The 'pounding' rhythm ('thump, thump' etc) could be said by a chorus, and the different lines by individual children. A variety of other sound effects could be added.

Working on an oil rig
The wind is howling,
Thump smash.
The waves are pounding,
Thump crash.
The drill is screaming,
Thump slash.
The men are shouting,
Thump dash.
The pumps are throbbing,
Thump clash.
The weather's worsening,
Thump flash.
The noise is dreadful,
Thump bash.
Working

Thump
On
Thump
An
Thump
Oil
Thump
Rig.

Part 3
At this point in the service the emphasis and tempo could change. The bridge by which this is achieved could be provided by a short passage, spoken by a good reader.

Reader

Getting oil from the sea bed is one form of harvest. There are many others – men reap crops, catch fish, mine coal. At this time of the year we give thanks for the gifts of the earth, and express gratitude to those who harvest them for us. Listen to this very old poem about harvesting crops in the English countryside long ago.

'Come forth, my Lord, and see the Cart,
Drest up with all the country art.
See here a Mankin, there a sheet;
The horses, mares and frisking fillies
(Clad all in linen, white as lillies).
The harvest swains and wenches bound
For joy, to see the Hock cart* crown'd'.
                                        Robert Herrick

*(The Hock cart was the one which brought the last load of corn from the fields).

Speaker   This is also a time when we should think
              of those thousands of people in parts of
              the world where there is never enough to
              eat. Listen to the following:

A tiny body
That cannot grow
Cries out for help.
Food and drink
And loving care
Are desperately needed.
This
Food
And Drink
And Care
Is needed
Not next month,
Not next week,
Not tomorrow,
But
Now!

Prayers
                    Let us give thanks for
                    The harvests of the earth
                    And those who reap them
                    on land and sea.
                    Let us pray for
                    Those who never have enough to eat
                    And for whom there is never the joy
                    Of harvest.
                    Father hear our prayers.
                        Amen

Hymn
'When God made the Garden of Creation' (*Come and Praise* Vol 1, 16).

'I WAS THERE'

Theme Easter

Calendar location March/April

Preparation
The basis of this assembly is a playscript in which a reporter interviews people who were present in Jerusalem at the time when Jesus was arrested.

It would add to the drama of the occasion if some visual and aural material supplemented the reading of the script by the presenters.

If an overhead projector is available then a running sequence of pictures drawn on transparencies might enhance the dramatic readings. A tape – recording of suitable music could be played in the background.

Narrator	This morning we are travelling to Jerusalem to hear something about the events of the first Easter. Here are the characters you will meet.
(*Characters step forward in turn and introduce themselves*)	
Bathsheba	My name is Bathsheba. I have lived in Jerusalem for many years.
Eli	I'm Eli. I help keep the city's streets clean.
Julius	I'm one of the Roman guard, at the Garden of Gethsemane. I'm called Julius.
Mary	Hello, I'm Mary. I'm a waitress.
Laertes	I'm called Laertes, my master is the Roman Governor Pontius Pilate.
Narrator	One of the most important functions of ECHO – the Time/Space television

programme, is to send its interviewers back in time to interview people who were present at important events in history. For today's programme one of our interviewers is in Jerusalem in the year 33. He is talking to a panel of people who observed some of the sensational events which took place there recently.

Interviewer   Good morning ladies and gentlemen. Today we are in Jerusalem. Surrounded by steep slopes on three sides, this 'city of peace' has seen some unusual and dramatic events recently. I am here to talk to some people who were present when they happened.

Interviewer   Now Bathsheba, I understand you have lived in Jerusalem all your life. Can you tell us something about the city?

Bathsheba   Well, as you know, the city is surrounded by walls. There are eight gateways, and just outside the walls is the Garden of Gethsemane.

Interviewer   Has the city been in existence long?

Bathsheba   Oh yes, hundreds of years – including the great time when David was king.

Interviewer   Is it a pleasant place in which to live?

Bathsheba   Yes and no. It has a great history – but who would like to be ruled by Roman governors, I ask you?

Interviewer	Hmmm, and I suppose this is one of the reasons why people got excited when they heard Jesus was coming.
Bathsheba	You could say that. After all, there were rumours of him being a new king.
Interviewer	Eli – I believe at the time of Jesus Christ's arrest you were still working at your job of keeping the streets clean?
Eli	Indeed I was – still am, in fact. I've never seen a day like that one when he came into the city.
Interviewer	Can you tell us something about it?
Eli	Well for a start a lot of Jesus' friends had come up from Galilee before him. They told everybody here that he was coming.
Interviewer	And. . .?
Eli	The folks here started to go mad – my lovely clean streets! They hacked off branches from every palm tree in sight and spread them on the road
Interviewer	Why did they do that?
Eli	You know the old superstition – palm trees are supposed to be a sign of victory, so people spread them ready for Jesus' victorious entry into the city.
Interviewer	I expect you were annoyed by the mess.
Eli	At first perhaps, but there was this terrific feeling of joy and enthusiasm. And then when everybody saw Jesus

coming on a donkey and the cheering started . . . I just joined in and shouted 'Hosannah' with the rest of them.

Interviewer   Unfortunately it didn't take long for things to change from joy to sorrow. Can you tell us anything about that, Julius?

Julius   I'm just a simple Roman soldier, you know, but there were rumours of a plot to trap this Jesus Christ.

Interviewer   I believe you actually saw this plot being put into action?

Julius   Almost by accident really.

Interviewer   Can you give us more details?

Julius   My job was to stand guard on the Garden of Gethsemane. The governor wanted to be sure nobody got up to any mischief there, so every night a guard patrolled the area. Anyway, this particular night I was on duty when Jesus Christ turned up with his friends.

Interviewer   What happened?

Julius   Noting much at first. They talked, most of them went to sleep, and then I was suddenly aware that about 50 of my mates from the 4th Legion had arrived. They hid in the bushes, and then one of this so called troublemaker's friends went up and kissed him. This was a signal and the 4th Legion moved in to make arrests.

Interviewer   Who said Jesus Christ was a trouble maker?

Julius   One of his own people, believe it or not – a High Priest called Caiaphas.

Interviewer   Viewers will know from reports at the time that Jesus Christ was arrested and taken to the High Priest's house for questioning. In the skirmish however, Peter, Jesus' closest friend escaped. Mary can tell us something about this.

Mary   True, I can. I work as a waitress and I was in the Garden of Gethsemane that night when all the trouble occurred. When Jesus was arrested the man who I now know was called Peter went mad – ready to fight the whole Roman army, he was.

Interviewer   What happened?

Mary   Jesus calmed him down before the soldiers took him to the High Priest's house. By now there was quite a crowd and everybody followed the action.

Interviewer   How do you mean?

Mary   Well the crowd went to the High Priest's house too.

Interviewer   And. . .

Mary   They couldn't get in, of course, so they

were all milling around in the courtyard outside. That was when I saw Peter again. He was standing by a fire in the courtyard.

Interviewer   Did anybody else recognise him?

Mary   They certainly did. While I watched, first one girl, then another girl, then a man from the crowd all came and said they recognised him.

Interviewer   What did he do?

Mary   Strange really – he yelled and shouted and said he knew nothing about Jesus. When he had done this for the third time it was nearly dawn and a cock began to crow. When he heard this Peter just burst into tears and ran out of the courtyard.

Interviewer   Of course, viewers, we all know that Jesus was brought to trial. Laertes here was present at that trial, where some very strange things happened.

Laertes   I work directly for Pontius Pilate, the Roman Governor. He wasn't very pleased about this business I can tell you.

Interviewer   Why was that?

Laertes   For a start Jesus did not behave like a guilty man at all. He made no pleas or protests – nothing.

Interviewer   Why didn't Pilate release him then – if he thought he was innocent?

Laertes	Ah – I know he wanted to. In fact he even offered to release Jesus. But those Jews went mad when he made this offer. 'Crucify him,' they shouted.
Interviewer	But surely Pilate was the governor – he could do what he liked?
Laertes	Perhaps – but he didn't want a riot on his hands. So he sent me to get a bowl of water. Then he washed his hands in this water and said to the crowd: 'My hands are clean of this man's blood.'
Interviewer	But he still handed Jesus over to Caiaphas and his plotters.
Laertes	Well, yes he did.
Interviewer	And so Jesus was taken and crucified.
Narrator	So ladies and gentlemen, we return to the ECHO studios of today. Our Time/Space interviewer in Jerusalem will no doubt have raised many questions you want to talk about between yourselves – especially when you think about what has happened since these events.

'Should I. . .?

Theme Making decisions

Calendar location
Possibly July as a 'leavers' service' but no other calendar significance.

Preparations
It may be helpful to rehearse the dramatic situations which make up most of the assembly. Some simple props might also be an asset, depending on what is available, eg brown shoes, a torn book.

Prepare three large placards, as follows:

1 | The robbers might still be about.
It could be a trap.
It is best to mind your own business.

2 | This man is too heavy to lift.
He's too badly injured to help anyway.
Where could I take him?

3 | This man is in trouble. I must help him the best way I can.

Part 1
This assembly focuses on something which everybody is faced with during their lives – making decisions. By means of story and drama it progresses from 'everyday' decisions to those which are much more difficult to make.

Speaker 1   Good morning everybody . . . first of all we are going to the Simmons household where Julie and Dawn are getting ready to go to a party.

Dawn	I'm going to put my red dress on.
Julie	But you've only got that pair of brown shoes.
Dawn	Well, a red dress goes with brown shoes, doesn't it?
Julie	No I don't think it does. Why don't you put your green dress on – that goes better with brown shoes.
Dawn	But my green dress isn't ironed.
Julie	Oh – and we have to go in ten minutes.
Dawn	What shall I wear? What shall I do?

Speaker 2   Dawn was trying to make a decision. Although it seemed an important one to her at the time, it doesn't seem important compared with other decisions which have to be made. Listen to the following story.

Speaker 3   It happened in the classroom last year. The teacher held up a reading book. It was open and a page had been torn out of the middle. The teacher was furious. 'Who did it?' she asked.
Nobody answered.
Then she began to go round everybody in the class saying.
'Wayne, did you do it? Scott did you do it? Kelly did you do it?'

Everybody said No and Mrs Dawkes got even more annoyed.

'Right,' she said. 'It's playtime now and I'm going to send everybody out. Anybody who knows *anything* about the tearing of this book can come and see me during playtime. If I don't hear anything there will be no more playtimes this week . . . or next week. We'll just sit silently in here every playtime until I find out who has done it.'

It was quieter than usual as we filed out into the playground. I caught Simon Groves looking at me. He was the biggest, toughest, roughest boy in the class – and he knew I had seen him tear the page out of the book.

Speaker 1   This time making a decision was much more difficult for all sorts of reasons. What would *you* have done? Perhaps you might think about this and talk about it in class after assembly.

Speaker 2   Now . . . look at our next presentation. As you do so think about the decisions which had to be made here.

Part 2: The Good Samaritan

At this part of the assembly the story of the Good Samaritan is acted out with supporting comment from a narrator. The three cards are introduced as indicated in the script.

Narrator	A man was once going from Jerusalem to Jericho. He had reached a lonely part of the road when he was suddenly attacked by bandits. *Action*
Narrator	The robbers left the man half dead at the side of the road. A priest came by soon afterwards. He saw the injured man but went by on the other side. *Action*
Narrator	Perhaps the priest thought these things before making his decision. *Show placard 1.*
Narrator	Some time after the priest went by, a Temple caretaker came along. He looked at the injured man and then decided to move on. *Action*
Narrator	Perhaps the Temple caretaker thought these things before making his decision. *Show placard 2.*
Narrator	Shortly afterwards a foreigner – a Samaritan – came along the road. He saw the injured man, stopped, bandaged his wounds, put him on his horse and

took him to an inn. He gave the inn-keeper some money, told him to look after the man and said if more money was needed he would give it on the way back.
Action

Narrator   Perhaps the foreigner thought the following when he made his decision.
Show placard 3.

Part 3

Speaker 1   We have seen in our presentation so far that making a decision is not an easy thing to do. Christians believe that they can often be guided in the decisions they make by readings from the Bible and by prayer. The following words are taken from the Book of Job:

Have I let the brambles grow where the wheat is? Have I thought about the needs of other people? Have I thought that money was all important? Have I gloated about how well off I am? Have I enjoyed unpleasant things happening to people I don't like?

Speaker 2   Christians believe that thinking about questions like this helps them to make the best decisions they can. We are now going to hear a very old Christian prayer. Say it a line at a time, after me:

'God be in my head, And in my understanding
Pause for response
God be in my eyes, And in my looking
Response
God be in my mouth, and in my speaking
Response
God be in my heart, And in my thinking.
Response

The assembly could then be ended by singing: 'The wise may bring their learning' (*Come and Praise* Vol 1, Number 64)

Signposts

Theme Showing the way

Calendar location
Any time of the year

Preparation
This assembly would be greatly enhanced by good visual displays of signposts, signs and symbols. Reading through the script will indicate what is needed for the actual assembly (road sign showing falling rocks, key or keys etc), but this need not be restrictive and there is a great deal of scope for extra development here.

Children who are 'signposts' should either carry a sign, or wear a hat or costume to indicate what they are – police officer, doctor, etc.

Part 1

Speaker	Our assembly begins with a short play. The Parker family is going on holiday. They have hired a caravan in a hilly part of Wales. They are driving to the caravan now. Listen to the conversation going on in the car. *The Parker family: Mr and Mrs Parker, Floella and Marcus, are arranged in chairs to appear as if in a car.*
Marcus	How long before we get there?
Mr Parker	Only about half an hour or so. Be patient.
Floella	I can't wait!
Mrs Parker	Well you'll have to wait a bit longer, won't you?

Marcus	Hey Dad – look at that sign ahead.
	Show sign: Danger – falling rocks.
Floella	It shows rocks falling – does it mean we can't go on?
Mr Parker	No, its not a sign which forbids us to go on – its a sign which warns us.
Marcus	You mean rocks are going to fall on us?
Mrs Parker	No, that's very unlikely.
Mr Parker	Perhaps we'll see a few rocks lying on the roadside. The sign really means take extra care.
Floella	Aren't warning signs a good idea?
Mrs Parker	They certainly are – in many ways.
Speaker	You can see from this short play that the sign we have seen here is one of warning. There are other signposts in life . . . but we'll leave that to Group 2.

Part 2
Pupils enter, one carrying a large bunch of keys.

Speaker 1	You have all seen a bunch of keys before.
Speaker 2	A key is something which opens a door . . . or a box . . . or a gate.
Speaker 3	Two saints have Keys as 'signposts' to help us remember them.

Speaker 4   These keys remind us not only of the saints but what they stand for. Take St Martha, for instance . . .

Speaker 1   She is the saint of good housekeeping. If you see a picture of her she will have a bunch of keys hanging from her belt.

Speaker 2   They show that she takes care of everything to do with our homes.

Speaker 3   St Peter is sometimes shown with one key, sometimes with a bunch of keys. His keys are to open the gates of Heaven.

Speaker 4   St Peter's keys show him to be taking care of people.

Speaker 1   Now I wonder what Group 3 have to tell us?

Part 3

Chorus   Our signposts are people. Here they are . . . there's a mum, a dad, a teacher, a doctor, a police officer.
As each of these people is mentioned a child steps forward to represent them. Once they are all in place each speaks.

Mum	I suppose I am a sort of signpost to my children. I try to help them by pointing out what's good for them, like eating good food . . .
Dad	. . . and going to bed early and getting plenty of sleep . . .
Mum	. . . and remembering things like good manners . . .
Dad	. . . and helping mums and dads occasionally!
Teacher	I am a signpost that points towards learning. It is a great help if we can all read and write, and the more knowledge we have the better equipped we are to enjoy life and make the most of it.
Doctor	If I was a signpost I would have HEALTH written on me. I try to point people into ways which keep them healthy, and I try to help them recover if they are ill.
Police officer	I am a signpost that points towards the sort of good behaviour which keeps law and order. This is the way to come for protection and help too.
Chorus	Now Group 4 are going to show you some signposts which need no words and no pictures.

Part 4

The children from Group 4 then enter and take turns to make a number of signs with their hands. These might include, in this order:

- a hand pointing
- a hand shake
- a 'thumbs up' sign
- a hand held up in a 'stop' signal
- a hand indicating 'go lower'
- a hand indicating 'go higher'
- hands indicating length (of a fish etc)
- a threatening fist
- a finger beckoning
- a hand waving farewell

Finally, all together, the children join their hands as in prayer.

Speaker   Our assembly this morning has been about signs which help us through life. Many people find prayer very helpful. Put your hands together in the sign for prayer and listen to the following Christian prayer:
Let us learn to
Give and not count the cost,
Work and not look for rest,
Not always be concerned about the reward.
(adapted from St Ignatius)

The assembly might be concluded by the singing of: 'One more step along the road I go' (*Come and Praise* Vol 1, 47)

Further sources

This could be followed up with a display of signs and symbols round the school. In this context *The Highway Code* would be useful. There are also good illustrations and comment in *Signs and Symbols* by Olivia Bennett, published by Unwin Hyman.

Labels

Theme Awareness of individual people

Calendar location
Any time

Preparation
The main visual aids required are four large, clearly-lettered labels:
OLD
HANDICAPPED
RELIABLE
HEROIC

These have to be brought to the front of the presenting group and it might be helpful for pupils to rehearse doing this a few times.

Other useful items associated with each of the presentations will need to be collected, ie objects depicting old age, pictures for the Archie MacFarlane story, tennis equipment.

Presentation
Begin with the presenting class marching to their staging area accompanied by some appropriately rousing music. They are carrying what appear to be large, rolled-up paper banners. Once in position these 'banners' are unfurled as each part of the action takes place.

Part 1
The 'Old' label is displayed. Then two or three children step out from the group holding various items which are synonymous with 'old'. One might hold up a stick and a pair of glasses, another a hearing aid and two or three cardigans.

Speaker One of the labels we attach to people is 'old.' What picture does this conjure up in your minds? Somebody who perhaps needs glasses, a hearing aid, a stick, lots of woollies to keep out the cold? Well, first of all we are going to tell you about a man

	called Archie. We'd like you to look at some pictures.
	Five children step forward. Each in turn holds up a picture, to portray a sequence of events.
Picture 1	This picture shows two men about to jump out of an aeroplane.
Picture 2	My picture shows them falling towards earth. They are doing a free-fall parachute jump – which means that they don't open their parachutes until they are falling at a very high speed.
Picture 3	My picture shows the two men just about to land on the ground. Their parachutes are still billowing out above them. They have fallen 12,000 feet through the sky.
Picture 4	This picture shows John, who is a parachute training instructor, and one of the men who made this jump.
Picture 5	This picture shows the other man who made the jump. His name is Archie and he got into the Guinness Book of Records for making this jump.
Speaker	You are probably wondering why Archie's name went into the Guinness Book of Records. Well, when he made this parachute jump he was 89 years of age – the oldest person ever to achieve such a feat.

Part 2

Children with the OLD label retreat into the background and those holding the HANDICAPPED label move to the front.

Speaker	One of the things handicapped people most want is to be treated 'normally' and on equal terms by those who have no handicaps. *One of the children holds up a tennis racquet. Then taking a tennis ball she bounces it several times on the racquet. (Pre-assembly rehearsal will have revealed which children are able to do this, and helped them perfect the skill.)*
Speaker	You might wonder what link there is between handicaps and tennis. That is why we are going to tell you the story of Doris. The story of Doris *The characters are: Narrator, Doctor, Mr and Mrs Hart, Doris, Tennis coach*
Narrator	This morning we are going to present a play about a girl called Doris Hart. The play begins when Doris was a small child.
Doctor	Ah, Mr and Mrs Hart, I've sent for you because I would like to talk about Doris.
Mrs Hart	Doris? It's not serious, is it Doctor? What's wrong with her?
Mr Hart	Keep calm, dear. I'm sure the doctor will tell us.

Doctor	I'm afraid it *is* serious. Doris is suffering from a disease called polio. It is affecting her legs badly and it is possible that she will be a cripple all her life.
Mr Hart	Can't you do anything?
Doctor	That's the worst part, I'm afraid. It may be necessary for us to take off one of Doris's legs because it is affected so badly.
Mrs Hart	No! I want you to try every other possible form of treatment rather than that. That must surely be the last resort.
Doctor	We'll certainly try, but I felt I had to warn you of every possibility.
Narrator	The worst did not happen. Doris did not lose her leg. It remained very weak, however, and made life difficult for her because, more than anything else, she wanted to be a tennis player. *Action: Doris being coached by a tennis expert.*
Coach	Come on Doris, you must get to that ball.
Doris	I'm trying, but I just can't move my legs quickly enough.
Coach	Then what must you do?
Doris	I don't know – what?
Coach	You've got to *think* more. You're never going to be as fast as other players so you are going to have to think faster than they do. You must anticipate where every shot is

	going to be hit – which will give you that split second more to get yourself in position.
Doris	I'll try. Right – start hitting them at me again.
	Action: the two players mime 'hitting' balls back and forth to each other.
Coach	Better, better – now you are beginning to anticipate well.
Narrator	So Doris practised her tennis – and practised, and practised. She became so good that she beat all the local players and then became a well-known international. Her greatest moment came when she reached the Women's Singles Final at Wimbledon. There she beat her opponent 6–0; 6–0; to win the championship. Doris had certainly overcome her handicap.

Part 3
Once the HANDICAPPED presentation is finished the next label – RELIABLE could be brought forward.

Chorus	Every December a very important service is held in Westminister Abbey. This is called the Children of Courage Award Service and it is always attended by a member of the Royal Family.

Speaker 1   At this service several children are given awards for outstanding actions during the year.

Speaker 2   Some of these children receive awards for being reliable in a crisis. Some have alerted the rescue services to come and help parents or grandparents who were taken ill. Others have saved people from drowning, rescued them from burning buildings and, in one case, helped a child stranded on a rooftop.

Speaker 3   These children have proved that, in a crisis, they could be relied upon to take the correct action.

Part 4

The next, and final change of the assembly, could then take place as the retreating RELIABLE label is replaced by that which proclaims HEROIC. When this is in position a chorus could announce the beginning of a play. The St Alban story might be read by speakers in the background, whilst other presenters mime the action in the foreground.

Characters Alban, the Priest, a Roman soldier, a second and third Roman soldier, narrator.

Narrator   Hundreds of years ago the Romans ruled Britain. One of the most important towns in the country was called Verulanium. One of its most important citizens was a man called Alban. Alban, like everybody else in Verulanium, knew that the Emperor's soldiers were constantly searching the town for Christians. The Romans wanted to stamp out the religion. They executed any Christians they found. Alban had no strong feelings about Christians – he didn't know any, but he didn't hate them as some people did.

One cold, windy night Alban was sitting in front of his fire . . .

Alban	How nice it is to be warm on such a dreadful night. I feel sorry for those poor people who haven't a home.
	A knock on the door
Alban	I wonder who that can be?
	He goes to the door and opens it. A man in a cloak is standing outside.
Alban	Good Gracious . . . I've seen people in those cloaks before – you must be a Christian priest.
Priest	I am and I beg you to help me.
Alban	Help you? How can I do that?
Priest	The Roman soldiers are only minutes behind me. Please let me stay in your house for a day or two. I'll be safe here.
Alban	Stay in my house? But that's against the law. Why on earth should I break the law to shelter a Christian priest?

Priest	I am not afraid for myself, but I have so much work to do. One less priest is one fewer person to tell the people of Verulanium the good news.
Alban	Well . . . all right. Come in and we'll talk about it.
Narrator	And so Alban took the priest into his home. During the next two days the two men had many long talks. Alban came to admire the priest; he thought nothing of his own safety, but simply wanted to stay alive so that he could tell others about Christianity. Late one night, when Alban and the priest were deep in conversation, a thunderous knock rattled the door.
	Loud knock at door.
Priest	They've found me. I knew it was too good to last.
Alban	Wait – you say your work has only just begun.
Priest	Of course, my friend, you know that from our conversations. But thank you for your great kindness, now I must . . . .
	Another thunderous knock
Alban	Wait – give me your cloak.
Priest	But . . .
Alban	Don't argue – just keep up the good work! *Alban opens the door, dressed in the priest's cloak, pushes his way past the soldiers and runs away.*

Soldier 1	It's him!
Soldier 2	After him, lads!
Soldier 3	There's three of us, we're bound to catch him.
	The three soldiers chase, and catch, Alban.
Soldier 1	Now priest – a night in the cells for you.
Soldier 2	And the judge tomorrow.
Soldier 3	And then . . .
Narrator	And so Alban was brought before the Roman Official. In daylight he was recognised instantly. 'Alban,' the judge gasped, 'what on earth made you protect that priest? You're not a Christian. Tell me it was all a mistake and we'll forget about the whole thing.' Then, to the judge's surprise, Alban replied that his conversations with the priest had convinced him of one thing. He was now a Christian and would always remain one. Alban refused to change his mind – and he was executed. Verulanium eventually became known as St Albans, and a beautiful abbey stands there to remind us of Britain's first martyr and saint.

Conclusion

For the conclusion of the service the four labels could be brought to the fore-front again, and everyone asked to bow their heads in prayer. The following prayer might then be read:

Let us think this morning about labels. Let us not judge people by appearances but let us always be aware of the qualities, needs and hopes of others.

Let us try to be kind and reliable at all times, and let us give thanks for the inspiration shown to us by heroic people.

Amen

The assembly could then be ended by everyone singing: 'The family of man' (*Come and Praise* Vol 1, 69)

Section C
Information for teachers

The school/Christian year

September

1 *Harvest* is the main Christian festival associated with this month. It is usually observed at the end of the month. The custom of displaying fruit, vegetables, flowers etc in churches dates from the middle of the last century. Seaside and industrial areas often celebrate their particular 'harvest'. (See 'On an oil rig' on page 144.)

Traditionally, once the harvest was gathered in, a 'Harvest home' was celebrated with a special supper. The last of the corn was shaped into a corn dolly. This was retained during the winter and sown with the new corn in anticipation of a good harvest. The corn dolly often appeared at the harvest service before being kept in a barn.

Harvest could yield many associated assembly themes. (*Food, giving and receiving, ways of saying 'thank you', celebration, conservation, rain, industry, the earth.*) There is also the 'Third World' aspect of failed harvests and famine – and what attempts are made to help in this situation.

2 Assemblies appropriate to this month are: 2, 5, 29, 46, 52, 59 'On an oil rig'.

3 The following dates offer opportunities for stimulating assemblies:

6th Pilgrim Fathers sailed from Plymouth (*Travel, customs, courage, 'into the unknown', persecution.*)

14th Holy Rood Day. 'Rood' is another name for 'cross'. In the 4th century Saint Helena supposedly found the cross on which Jesus was crucified. (*Stories of Jesus, saints.*)

19th Death of Dr Barnardo in 1905

29th St Michael's Day. The Archangel Michael is usually portrayed as the conqueror of Lucifer, the rebel angel. (*Good and evil, light and darkness, justice.*)

October

There are no major Christian festivals during October, but several interesting saints might be featured (see below)

Linked assemblies

Assemblies appropriate to this month are: 10, 14, 32, 34, 40.

Notable dates

4th Death of St Francis. A rich young man who gave away his property after illness, Francis dedicated the rest of his life to helping others. His association with animals grew from his taming of a savage wolf which was killing both

other animals and men. (*Animals, caring, self-sacrifice, spirit of service, pets.*)
   18th St Luke's Day (*Writers, doctors, books, words.*)
   25th St Crispin's Day – patron saint of shoemakers (*Jobs, working for others, the need to share skills, varied talents, feet, hands.*)

November
All Saints' Day (1st November) is the time when saints and martyrs (particularly those without a 'day' of their own) are remembered. One source of the day's origin stems from the 7th century when the famous Roman temple, the Pantheon, was converted and consecrated as a place of Christian worship. (*People, families, ancestors, change, contrasts.*)
   All Souls' Day, which follows, is a time when Christians remember all those who have died. In the past, special 'soul cakes' (small, flat cakes with spices added) were eaten by families as part of the 'remembering' activities. (*Families, memories, the past, learning from the past, good deeds.*)
   Advent begins in November (*Light, preparations, churches, beginnings, signs and symbols, worship.*)

Linked assemblies
Assemblies appropriate to this month are: 18, 19, 26, 31, 50; 'Labels'.

Notable dates
11th Remembrance Day (*War, peace, forgiveness, brave acts, 'one family,' waste.*)
   11th St Martin's Day – the saint who tore his cloak to give half to a beggar – later seeing in a dream that the beggar was Jesus. (*Rich and poor, generosity, values.*)
   22nd St Cecilia's Day – patron saint of music and musicians. (*Ears, fingers, talents, senses, beauty, sounds, music.*)
   30th St Andrew's Day – patron saint of Scotland, brother of Simon Peter, supposedly the apostle who found the boy with the loaves and fishes in the famous 'feeding of the five thousand' story. (*Food, neighbours, determination, loyalty, miracles.*)

December
Primary school teachers need no reminding about how much Christmas dominates those last weeks in December before the end of term. As such it is sometimes a good idea to have a series of assemblies which examine some of the many different aspects of Christmas.
   These might include:

- A more detailed look at the original 'Santa Claus' – St Nicholas, Bishop of Myra. A man of wisdom and generosity, he died in 342. His 'day' is the *6th*.
- Christmas customs – plays, feasts, songs, carols, trees, presents.
- Christmas creatures – cock, robin, ox, ass.
- History – festivities banned by Puritans in 1642; Christmas made a fast day in 1644; Victorian influence – cards etc.
- Writings – Dickens, Shakespeare, Laurie Lee, Bible, poems.
- Christmas in different parts of the world.
- Links with other religions, particularly 'Festivals of Light' such as Divali, Hanukkah.
- Considerations of giving and receiving – friends, family, neighbours, those who may be forgotten at this time of the year.

Linked assemblies
Assemblies appropriate to this month are: 12, 27, 39, 41, 42, 51.

Notable dates
For those who seek some variety from the Christmas theme there are some other interesting possibilities earlier in the month.

1st St Elgin's Day. An unusual saint in that his patronage includes such various groups of people as miners, cab drivers, farmers and jockeys. (*Different jobs, different talents, working together, appreciating others.*)

10th There are two possibilities for this date. Alfred Nobel, founder of the famous prizes (physics, medicine, chemistry, literature, service of peace) died in 1896. (*Prizes, rewards, values, mankind, great people.*)

This is also the date on which, in 1948, the United Nations agreed to the Universal Declaration of Human Rights:

'All human beings are born free and equal in dignity and rights. They are endowed with reason and conscience and should act towards one another in a spirit of brotherhood.' (*Conscience, rules, countries, power, fairness, justice.*)

January
The 6th of the month sees the celebration of the Feast of the Epiphany. Twelve days after Christmas, this commemorates the day the three Kings arrived in Bethlehem with their gifts of gold, frankincense and myrrh for the baby Jesus.

Orthodox Christian churches celebrate Christmas on this day. An appealing story for primary children concerns the fact that on this feast French children eat a marzipan-covered fruit cake (rather like our Christmas cake) which has a single almond inside it. Whoever gets the almond in their slice is in charge of the home for the day. (*Gifts, journeys, special occasions, parties.*)

Linked assemblies
Assemblies appropriate to this month are: 16, 21, 22, 47.

Notable dates
3rd Birth of J R R Tolkien in 1892 (*Stories, reading, words.*)
4th Birth of Jacob Grimm in 1785 (*Joy, morals, talents.*)
14th Birth of Albert Schweitzer (see Assembly 21)
17th St Anthony's Day – patron saint of domestic animals. (*Pets, pet care, animal rights, responsibilities, companionship.*)

Februrary
February 2nd is Candlemas – the occasion which celebrates the presentation of Jesus in the temple at Jerusalem. Candles of churches are blessed for the whole year on this day. They symbolize the Biblical comment that Jesus was to be 'a light to lighten the Gentiles'. (Luke 2:32). (*Light, celebration, children, guidance.*)

Shrovetide is the time before Lent which is associated with feasting. Collop Monday was a time when fried meat was eaten.

Shrove Tuesday saw fats and butter used up in pancakes. *Shrove Tuesday* is the 41st day before Easter. *Ash Wednesday* is the first day of Lent. The latter is a day of great solemnity, on which members of church congregations are daubed with ashes to remind them of their sins. (*Sacrifice, meditation, going without, concentration, mistakes, helping.*)

Linked assemblies
Assemblies appropriate to this month are: 7, 24, 37, 48, 49, 55.

Notable dates
14th St Valentine's Day. This offers a great deal of scope for assemblies. (*Love, marriage, gifts, communications, secrets.*)

March
Bearing in mind that Easter is a moveable feast, Lent continues into March. Use might be made of the following adaptation of a 6th century prayer at this time:

Almighty God, without you we have no power to help ourselves. Protect both our bodies and our minds at this time. Cleanse us from evil deeds and evil thoughts. Amen.

Mothering Sunday is the fourth Sunday in Lent. Traditionally this was the day on which apprentices were given leave to visit their mothers. Violets and simnel cake were traditional gifts on this occasion. Modern children enjoy this opportunity to thank their mothers. (*Mothers, children, families, cooking, worries, traditions.*)

Linked assemblies
Assemblies appropriate to this month are: 4, 8, 9, 11, 20; 'Signposts'.

Notable dates
St David (*1st*) and St Patrick (*17th*) have their 'days' during March.

2nd John Wesley, the founder of Methodism, died in 1791;

4th, 1824 what eventually became the Royal National Lifeboat Institution was founded.

All of these events are useful assembly starting points (*Saints, great deeds, great men, courage of different kinds, determination, dedication*).

April
Passion Sunday, which follows Mothering Sunday, reminds us of Jesus' suffering in the Garden of Gethsemane; *Palm Sunday* celebrates the entry into Jerusalem. The Thursday of Holy Week is *Maundy Thursday*, when the Last Supper is remembered. The crucifixion on *Good Friday* is followed by the resurrection on *Easter Day*.

The large candle which is ceremonially lit in churches on Easter Day symbolises new life – as does the originally secular tradition of giving Easter eggs.

For assemblies to do with Easter a useful link of words and letters with top juniors can be effective using subjects like 'passion' and 'compassion'.

Linked assemblies
Assemblies appropriate for this month are: 15, 30, 43, 44, 56; 'I was there'.

Notable dates
Saints' days this month include St George (*23rd*) and St Mark (*25th*).

April Fools' Day offers scope for appreciation of humour – and the need to laugh with people and not at them.

10th birth of William Booth, founder of the Salvation Army in 1829.

15th the sinking of the *Titanic* on 15th in 1912. All these offer assembly ideas. (*Values, awe, man's conceit, compassion, rich – poor, being prepared, the power of Nature.*)

May
Whitsuntide commemorates the birth of the Christian Church. It falls on the Jewish Feast of Pentecost and is the time when the followers of Jesus were encouraged by the Holy Spirit. As a result they went out into the world

spreading the message and starting the growth of Christianity. (*Inspiration, communication, growth, 'spreading a message'.*)

Three Rogation days precede *Ascension Day*. These were times when special prayers were said for the harvest.

Linked assemblies
Assemblies appropriate to this month are: 3, 17, 28, 33, 35, 53, 60.

Notable dates
1st St James' Day. James supposedly bore a great resemblance to Jesus. The kiss which Judas gave Jesus in the Garden of Gethsemane was a means of identification which this resemblance made necessary.

8th Red Cross Day

26th is St Augustine's Day. Augustine established a monastery at Canterbury – this is now the site of the cathedral.

June
June is not a significant month in the Christian year, but a particularly useful occasion for assembly purposes is *World Children's Day* on the 15th.

Approximately half the world's population is made up of children under 15, and many of these have lives of hardship and suffering. Because of this the United Nations General Assembly set aside one day a year to focus on these children's needs. Two organisations particularly concerned with this issue are Save the Children Fund and UNICEF (United Nations Childrens' Fund). (*Children, Third World, suffering, giving, helping, practical, concerns, other countries, barriers, peace.*)

Linked assemblies
Assemblies which are appropriate for this month are: 1, 6, 23, 25, 45, 57.

Notable dates
Three important saints' days this month are St Alban (*22nd*); St John the Baptist (*24th*); St Peter (*29th*). Another useful date is the *27th*, on which date Helen Keller was born in 1880 (*handicaps, those who care for us, gifts of healing*).

July
Without major significance in the Christian year, July was the month in which churches were thoroughly cleaned and dry rushes spread on the floor. Traditionally the 27th was the day on which Noah released a dove from the

Ark. (*Rules, punishments, hope, beginnings.*)
St Swithin's Day on the *15th* and St Christopher's Day on *25th* both offer interesting assembly possibilities.
Assemblies appropriate to this month are: 13, 36, 38, 54, 58; 'Should 1'?

Themes

Sometimes during the school year it is useful to group a number of assemblies together to reflect a particular theme.

The assemblies in this book could be grouped in a number of themes, as indicated below. The theme title is followed by the appropriate assembly number.

Theme	Assembly numbers
Ambitions	1, 15, 16, 35, 46.
Animals	10, 14, 34, 48, 49.
Asking questions	22, 23, 29, 34, 45.
Barriers	1, 9, 24, 29, 38, 46, 50.
Beauty	25, 30, 33, 59.
Beginnings	14, 21, 31, 32, 49, 59.
Caring	10, 18, 19, 21, 23, 24, 34, 41, 50.
Change	12, 17, 27, 41, 50.
Communication	9, 21, 29, 45, 53.
Concern	2, 12, 19, 29, 44, 51.
Courage	3, 9, 13, 15, 20.
Danger	6, 11, 13, 18, 20, 53.
Determination	1, 15, 16, 45, 50.
Discovery	16, 22, 26, 32, 33.
Duty	11, 17, 21, 34, 40, 41, 53.
Environment	2, 19, 21, 25, 27, 29, 59.
Failure	7, 17, 35, 36, 38.
Faith	8, 49, 50, 53, 54, 59, 60.
Family	4, 8, 12, 14, 39, 41, 46, 47, 51, 52.
Food	5, 29, 47, 48, 52, 59.
Foolishness	5, 17, 20, 31, 36, 40, 44, 48, 51.
Friendship	10, 19, 23, 31, 55.
Generosity	19, 37, 39, 41, 42, 47, 51, 54.
Growth	2, 22, 29, 49, 59.
Handicaps	1, 3, 9, 15, 29.
Home	4, 19, 31, 39, 47.
Hope	2, 3, 8, 21, 45, 50.

Journeys	8, 9, 11, 13, 16, 18, 20, 41, 60.
Joy	8, 14, 25, 33, 43, 47, 52, 56.
Justice	5, 27, 29, 34, 35, 37, 40, 48.
Living together	5, 17, 21, 23, 28, 31, 38, 39, 56.
Love	7, 19, 20, 24, 35, 41, 47, 51.
Machines	11, 13, 15, 40.
Names	26, 31, 37, 55.
Nature	8, 25, 30, 46.
Neighbours	4, 6, 18, 28.
Ourselves	13, 22, 23, 33, 38, 43.
Overcoming difficulties	1, 11, 15, 29, 53.
Patience	15, 39, 49.
Peace	31, 52.
Poverty	2, 19, 27, 29, 45.
Power	16, 27, 31, 34, 35, 37, 43, 52, 57.
Prayer	8, 29, 49, 50, 57, 60.
Rules	5, 27, 40, 44.
Seasons	11, 25, 29, 30, 33.
Senses	3, 15, 22, 25, 33, 56.
Talents	1, 3, 15, 37, 41.
Time	12, 22, 25, 27, 33.
Treasure	14, 29, 32, 45.
Values	11, 12, 17, 19, 20, 23, 35, 58.
Waste	24, 27, 40, 51.
Wisdom	21, 26, 32, 35, 44, 46, 57.
Words	15, 31, 35, 38, 39, 45.
Work	3, 15, 17, 27, 35, 38, 40, 46.

Age groupings

In the hands of experienced presenters these assembly stories and poems can be used right across the junior age range. If they are to be used 'instantly' – that is to say, read straight from the book, then it may be helpful to have an age grouping of the immediate suitability of the core material.

Obviously some of this core material is well suited to more than one age group, other examples are more specific. It is hoped that the following grouping arrangement may be helpful.

Age group   **Assembly numbers**
Lower juniors: 2, 3, 4, 5, 6, 13, 14, 22, 23, 25, 26, 27, 34, 36, 37, 38, 40, 41, 42, 43, 44, 45, 47, 48, 49, 55, 56, 58.

Middle juniors: 2, 3, 4, 5, 6, 9, 10, 11, 12, 13, 14, 16, 21, 22, 23, 25,
                         26, 27, 30, 32, 34, 36, 37, 38, 40, 41, 42, 43, 44, 45,
                         46, 47, 48, 49, 50, 53, 54, 55, 56, 58, 59.
Upper juniors: 1, 2, 3, 4, 5, 6, 7, 8, 9, 10, 11, 12, 13, 14, 15, 16, 17,
                         18, 19, 20, 21, 23, 25, 26, 27, 28, 29, 30, 31, 32, 33,
                         34, 35, 37, 39, 40, 43, 45, 46, 47, 50, 52, 53, 54, 55,
                         56, 58, 59, 60.

Sources

Hymns
All the hymns recommended in this book come from the BBC's *Come and Praise* books. Vol 1 has been a best seller for years now, and the last year has seen the addition of Vol 2.

Between them these books offer a total of 149 hymns. The selection is excellent and this is a resource which is well worth having.

Organisations
The following list is a rather selective one. The emphasis is on material which can be used directly for assemblies. This list is divided into two sections – religious and secular organisations.

Religious organisations
Christian Education Movement, 2 Chester House, London N10 1PR. (Tel 01 458 4366) This is an extremely valuable source of sound, practical material for both RE and assemblies. Regular supplies of documents and information can be obtained for a small annual subscription.

Christian Aid, PO Box, London SW9 8BH. (Tel 01 733 5500) During their 'week' in May some excellent assembly material is available. Leaflets, posters, film strips can also be obtained at any time. There are many local secretaries throughout the country and these can be very helpful.

RADIUS, The Religious Drama Society of Great Britain, St Paul's Church, Covent Garden, Bedford Street, London WC2E 9ED. (Tel 01 836 8669) RADIUS has an extensive collection of dramatic scripts of plays for all age groups. Single copies of these may be borrowed freely, sets must be hired.

United Society for the Propagation of the Gospel, USPG House, 15 Tufton Street, London SW1P 3QQ. (Tel 01 222 4222) Material from this source is only suitable for the top end of the junior school. There is however a wide variety of publications, film strips and audio-visual aids available. Enquiries should be made direct to the Schools and Children's Work Secretary.

Secular organisations
BBC School Radio and Television, School Broadcasting Council for the United Kingdom, The Langham, Portland Place, London W1A 1AA. Many teachers will know the RE and assembly material which emanates from the BBC. This is usually of a high quality and is always worth checking on an annual basis.

Centre for World Development, 128 Buckingham Palace Road, London W1. (Tel 01 730 8332) Useful for background information on world issues for top juniors.

The Conservation Trust, 246 London Road, Earley, Reading RG6 1AJ, (Tel 0734 663650) A useful source for material for assemblies concerned with Nature, Environment, Caring etc. The material spans the school years from 5 upwards.

Dr Barnardo's, Tanners Lane, Barkingside, Ilford, Essex 1G6, 1QG, (Tel 01 550 8822) Within the last year this organisation has produced a marvellous primary school pack with some really excellent assembly material in it. This should not be missed, and it is free!

Oxfam, 274 Banbury Road, Oxford OX2 7DZ. (Tel 0865 56777) A good source for evocative visual material.

Further visual aids
Philip Green Educational Ltd, 112a Alcester Road, Studley, Warwickshire B80 7NR. (Tel 0527 854711) have recently published several sets of packaged photographs, each with a linking poem. Subject titles of the packs include *Celebrations*, *Pets*, *School*, *Colors*, *Seasons* and *Weather*. The photographs are superb and the poems are often well suited to junior school assemblies (eg 'Blame' by Alan Ahlberg; 'Timothy Winters' by Charles Causley; 'The School Year' by Wes Magee.)
    Although this material has many curriculum uses it is exceptionally good value for assemblies.

Nature Conservancy Council, Northminster House, Peterborough PE1 1UA, (Tel 0733 40345)
    A source of some excellent posters which would fit in with many assemblies.